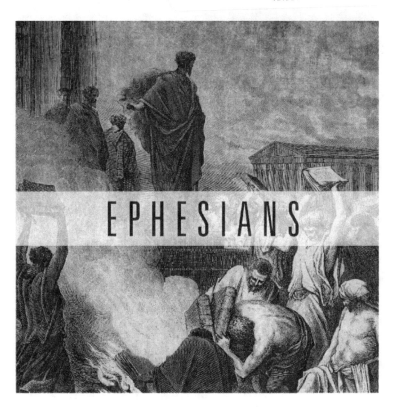

EPHESIANS

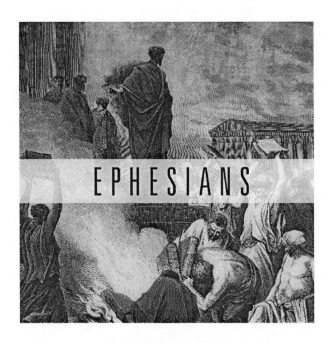

The Theology of
Paul's Epistle to the Ephesians

Brief Commentary and Study Guide

For
Personal Study and Bible Classes

By:
Dr. Ian A. Fair

HCU Media LLC
Accra, Ghana · Plano, TX

THE THEOLOGY OF PAUL'S EPISTLE TO THE EPHESIANS

A BRIEF COMMENTARY AND STUDY GUIDE ON PAUL'S LETTER TO THE EPHESIAN CHURCH

HCU Media LLC
www.HCUMedia.com

Published and Copyright © 2014
By Dr. Ian A. Fair & HCU Media LLC

ISBN-13: 978-1-939468-03-1 (Paperback Edition)

Also available in electronic book form– for more information reference our website: www.HCUMedia.com

Scripture quotations, unless otherwise noted, are from The Holy Bible,
Revised Standard Version, copyright 1971, Zondervan Bible Publishers.

Cover Design by Dale Henry – www.dalehenrydesign.com

First Edition January 2014
10 9 8 7 6 5 4 3 2 1

The Theology of Ephesians

CONTENTS

The Theology of Ephesians

Bibliography

The following resources have been used in preparing these study notes and are recommended for additional study:

Greek Lexicons (Dictionaries)
Friberg, Timothy, Barbara Friberg, Neva F. Miller, *Analytical Lexicon of The Greek New Testament.*
Kittel, Gerhard, Gerhard Friedrich, *Theological Dictionary of the New Testament.*
Zodhiates, Spiros, *The Complete Word Study Dictionary: New Testament.*

Please read Paul's Epistle to the Ephesians before you begin this study and the appropriate text before each lesson!

Dictionaries
The Anchor Bible Dictionary.
The International Standard Bible Encyclopedia.
Easton's Bible Dictionary.
Harper's Bible Dictionary.
The New Bible Dictionary.
Tyndale Bible Dictionary.
Baker Encyclopedia of the Bible.

Introductions to the New Testament
Fee, Gordon D. and Douglas Stuart, *How to Read the Bible Book by Book*, Zondervan, 2002.
Holladay, Carl R., *A Critical Introduction to the New Testament*, Abingdon, 2005.
Johnson, Luke Timothy, *The Writings of the New Testament*, Fortress, 1999.

Commentaries and Theological Studies

Arnold, Clinton E., *Ephesians: Exegetical Commentary on the New Testament*, Zondervan, 2011.

Barth, Marcus. *Ephesians*, Doubleday, 1974.

Bloesch, Donald G., *Essentials of Evangelical Theology*, Vol. 2, New York: Harper and Row, 1978.

Bruce, F. F. *The Epistle to the Ephesians,* London: Pickering and Inglis, 1961.

Bruce, F. F. *The Epistles to the Colossians, to Philemon, and to the Ephesians,* Wm. B. Eerdmans, 1984.

Caird, G. B. *Paul's Letters from Prison*, Oxford: Oxford University Press, 1976.

Foulkes, Francis. *Ephesians*, Tyndale New Testament Commentaries, William B. Eerdmans, 1989.

Gundry, Robert H. *Commentary on Ephesians*, Baker Academic, 2010.

Guthrie, Donald, *New Testament Theology,* Downers Grove: Inter-Varsity Press, 1981.

Lincoln, Andrew T. *Ephesians*, Word Biblical Commentary, Word Books, 1990.

Martin, Ralph P., *Ephesians, Colossians, and Philemon*, Interpretation, John Knox Press, 2012.

Norman Tom Wright, *Paul or Everyone, The Prison Letters*, SPCK, 2004.

O'Brian, Peter T., *The Letter to the Ephesians*, Wm. B. Eerdmans, 1999.

Richardson, Alan, *A Dictionary of Christian Theology*, London: SCM Press, 1969.

Lesson 1

General Introduction to the Prison Epistles
Ephesians, Philippians, Colossians, and Philemon

Note the following prescripts and salutations that introduce these four epistles:

Eph 1:1-2; *"Paul, an apostle of Christ Jesus by the will of God, To the saints who are also faithful in Christ Jesus: [2] Grace to you and peace from God our Father and the Lord Jesus Christ."*

Col 1:1-2; *"Paul, an apostle of Christ Jesus by the will of God, and Timothy our brother, [2] To the saints and faithful brethren in Christ at Colossae: Grace to you and peace from God our Father."*

Philemon vs. 1-3; *"Paul, a prisoner for Christ Jesus, and Timothy our brother, To Philemon our beloved fellow worker [2] and Apphia our sister and Archippus our fellow soldier, and the church in your house: [3] Grace to you and peace from God our Father and the Lord Jesus Christ."*

Phil 1:1-2; *"Paul and Timothy, servants of Christ Jesus, To all the saints in Christ Jesus who are at Philippi, with the bishops and deacons. [2] Grace to you and peace from God our Father and the Lord Jesus Christ."*

Note the similarities and differences in these salutations.

Note also that some translations of Ephesians (RSV) do not include the words "who are at Ephesus", or indicate in a footnote that this may have not been in many early manuscripts (NIV). This indicates that the letter originally may have been a circular letter written to several churches in the Roman province of Asia. The Greek manuscripts are divided on this. We will say more on this later in our study of the text.

Notice the interesting comment regarding bishops and deacons in Philippians. This kind of expression is not found elsewhere in the Pauline Epistles.

These epistles are called the Prison Epistles because they were most likely written by Paul when he was in prison in Rome for approximately 2 years toward the end of his ministry, ca. A.D. 60-62 or 61-63.

There are two other places mentioned by some scholars for the writing of the Prison Epistles; Ephesus and Caesarea Maritima (Caesarea on the Coast of the Ocean). However, Ephesus and Rome are the best attested places of origin. Rome is normally considered to be the traditional place of writing and seems the most likely provenance for these epistles.

The circumstances leading to Paul's imprisonment in Rome were as follows; at Miletus (Acts 20:17) Paul called the Elders of the church in Ephesus to meet with him. The text indicates that he would not see the elders of Ephesus again. Paul then left the Ephesian elders at Miletus and travelled toward Caesarea and Jerusalem (Acts 21:1-15). While in Jerusalem to deliver a benevolent gift from the Gentile churches to the church in Jerusalem (cf. 1 Cor 16:1; 2 Cor 8, 9; Rom 15:30) Paul was arrested (Acts 21:27) and was tried by the Sanhedrin (Acts 23:1). When the Jews made a plot to kill Paul a Roman Centurion transferred him to Caesarea to be tried by Felix, the Roman Governor of the region. Exercising his rights as a Roman citizen, Paul appealed his case to Caesar and was then shipped off to Rome. Carefully read Acts 24:1-25:12.

After arriving in Rome he was placed in prison or under house arrest until his accusers arrived from Jerusalem. He was released after two years (according to Roman law) when his accusers did not arrive to bring charges against him.

While in prison in Rome, Paul had plenty of time to contemplate his missionary experiences and his ministry. It is most likely that it was during this time that Paul wrote the four Prison Epistles. In due course Paul was released from the Roman prison and spent some time in house arrest. He was able to receive visitors to his house and to conduct a limited ministry of outreach.

One of his visitors was a minister from Colossae named Epaphras. Epaphras came to visit him to inform him of the church in Colossae. He most likely also told Paul of the work in Ephesus. This prompted Paul to write the letter to Colossae and possibly the one to Ephesus, which as I have already mentioned, was possibly a circular letter to churches in the region of Asia.

Another person Paul met and converted in Rome was Onesimus, a runaway slave from Colossae. Paul reluctantly sent him back to Philemon, a leader of the church in Colossae, with a letter which we know as Philemon; one of the four prison Epistles.

For some reason, possibly the receipt of a gift from the church in Philippi, Paul wrote the letter to the Philippian church toward the close of his two year imprisonment.

There are some scholars who question the Pauline authorship of Ephesians and Colossians, but this is not a universal opinion. These scholars consider either one or both Ephesians and Colossians to have been written by someone close to Paul, possibly by a fellow missionary.

The epistle regarding which most questions are raised is Ephesians. Reasons for questioning Ephesians are as follows; the impersonal nature of the epistle – it contains no personal greetings; the discussion relating to the church seems to manifest a later understanding and development of the church; a greater emphasis is given to the universal church; some of the language and terminology seems different from the accepted Pauline Epistles like Romans, Corinthians, and Galatians.

However, the fact that Ephesians was possibly not written to one congregation with specific problems and is seemingly a general or universal letter negates much of these arguments. We will notice the universal circular nature of Ephesians shortly in our detailed study of the Ephesian Epistle.

We will, however, work from the view that all four of these epistles are Pauline Epistles, written by the Apostle Paul while in a Roman prison. Cf. Luke Timothy Johnson, *The Writing of the New Testament*, 1999; Gordon D. Fee & Douglas Stuart, *How to Read the Bible Book by Book*, 2002; Norman Tom Wright, *Paul or Everyone, The Prison Letters*, 2004.

Three cities are involved in the four Prison Epistles; Ephesus, Colossae, and Philippi. The fourth letter, Philemon, was written to a church leader in the city of Colossae.

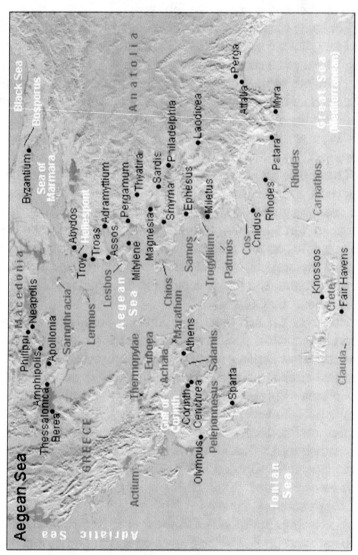

Map: Copyright of Manna, www.biblemaps.com
Used by permission of Manna.

The church in Ephesus was a leading church in the Roman Province of Asia; the other church at Colossae was a small church, possibly a house church. Colossae was also in the Roman Province of Asia. The Ephesian letter served as a circular letter intended for other churches in Asia but apparently addressed initially to the church in Ephesus since the church in Ephesus was a center of Pauline activity in Asia. The Roman Province of Asia is today Modern Western Turkey. A third epistle was written to the Philippian church; Philippi was located in the Roman Province of Macedonia. The letter to Philemon was a personal letter written to a church leader, Philemon, who was a member of the small church in the city of Colossae. See the map enclosed above to locate these cities; **Philippi** is toward the top center of the map; **Ephesus** is in the center of the map; **Colossae** unfortunately is not shown on the map but it was located about 3/4 inch to the right of Ephesus, just above Laodicea and below Philadelphia on the accompanying map.

Major Lessons to Learn from the General Introduction

- There are four Pauline Epistles grouped under the heading, Prison Epistles: Ephesians, Philippians, Colossians, and Philemon.
- They are called Prison Epistles because Paul was in prison when he wrote them, most likely in Rome.
- The first three are congregational letters; Philemon is a personal letter to a leader in the church in Colossae.
- The best date for these epistles is c.a. A.D. 60-62 or 61-63.

Questions and Discussion

- Can you picture in your mind's eye where the three cities of the Prison Epistles were located? One was in Macedonia. Which one? Where were the other two?
- Where was Philemon living when Paul wrote his letter to Philemon?
- From the salutations in Ephesians and Colossians how did Paul consider his apostleship?

- Why might Paul have needed to stress the point of his apostleship?
- What is the significance of Paul's apostleship to us in the church today?

Lesson 2

The City of Ephesus

Archaeological excavations show that the area around Ephesus was inhabited as early as the Neolithic age (6000 B.C.). In Paul's day it was an old and well established city.

Ephesus, now modern Selcuk, therefore had a long and impressive history. It already had a great cultural heritage and tradition when Paul arrived on the scene.

The ancient city itself was founded as an Attic-Ionian colony in the 10th century B.C. on the Ayasuluk Hill, three kilometers from the center of the present Selcuk (as attested by excavations at Selcuk during the 1990s). The mythical founder of the city was Androklos a prince of Athens, who had to leave his country after the death of his father. Androklos drove out most of the original native inhabitants of the area and united his people with those who remained.

By the time we encounter Ephesus in Paul's day it was a cosmopolitan city with a rich religious history and pagan undercurrent, heavily imbued with Greek mythology and the mystery religions. An incipient form of Gnosticism[1] pervaded the whole region of the Roman Province of Asia.

Ephesus was a major city, a prominent sea port on the Aegean Sea, and the head of the fertile Caicus Valley. At the time of Paul's arrival in Ephesus the city had already for many years been a major cultural, religious, and educational center for Asia.

Ephesus was dominated by the temple of Artemis, virgin Goddess of the Greeks. Artemis[2] was also the Hellenic Goddess of fertility, of the wilderness, forests, hills, and hunts. She was

---

[1] Gnosticism was a form of Platonism which primarily considered all physical matter to be evil. We will study Gnosticism in greater detail below.
[2] Artemis is sometimes referred to as the Roman goddess Diana but in the Greek speaking Asian world she was known as Artemis.

often depicted carrying a bow and arrows. She was the legendary daughter of the god Zeus, and twin sister of Apollo.

The temple to Artemis was considered one of the seven wonders of the ancient world. Legend has it that construction of the temple which took 120 years to complete was begun by Croesus of Lydia, c.a.550 B.C. It was dedicated to Artemis in 550 B.C. Over history, the temple was destroyed and rebuilt four times and was finally destroyed sometime in the 4th century AD.

The temple consisted of 127 beautiful white columns, each 60 feet in height; many of which were beautifully carved. The temple was 450 foot long and 225 foot wide.

The temple housed many fine artworks. Sculptures by renowned Greek artists adorned the temple. In addition, the temple was embellished with fine paintings and gilded columns of gold and silver. The sculptors often competed for opportunity to have their masterpieces installed in the temple. Many of these sculptures were of Amazons who are mythologically said to have founded the city of Ephesus. The temple columns were adorned by magnificent carved reliefs.

Legend has it that on July 21, 356 B.C., the night Alexander the Great was born, a psychopathic arsonist intent on immortality set fire to the temple. Plutarch remarked that Artemis was so preoccupied with Alexander's delivery that she failed to save her burning temple. The arsonist, Herostratus, was motivated by visions of fame regardless of the cost. The Ephesians were so outraged with Herostratus that they instructed that Herostratus' name should never be recorded in any chronicles and that anyone who spoke of him should be put to death.

Legend also records that twenty-two years later, during his sweep through Asia Minor, Alexander the Great offered to reconstruct the temple. In a famous refusal related by Strabo, the Ephesians said it wasn't right for one God to build a temple to another God.

The Temple was rebuilt several times following the original model of a raised platform, a feature of classical architecture adopted in the construction of later temples.

By 263 A.D., the temple was first plundered by Nero and later destroyed by the Goths.

The temple was again reconstructed in the 4th cent A.D., but the growing power and influence of Christianity in Ephesus eventually saw the demise of the temple and its influence. Much of the structural material was used to build the magnificent 6th cent A.D. basilica of St. John's on a nearby hill in Ephesus, and stones from the temple were also used to construct the Hagia Sofia, the magnificent Christian church in Istanbul. The Hagia Sofia was eventually converted into a museum by the Muslims after the 1453 Ottoman Turk defeat of the Christians in Constantinople.

The site of the temple of Artemis was rediscovered in 1869 on an expedition sponsored by the British Museum, and several artifacts and sculptures from the reconstructed temple can be seen in the local museum in Selcuk today.

The present day ruins of the temple to Artemis at modern day Selcuk (Ephesus) are hardly existent. All that remains is one reconstructed column and several large pieces of white marble.

Below is photo of an artist's impression of a statue erected to Artemis, a representation of which can also be seen in a square in modern Selcuk (Ephesus).

The Great Theater of Ephesus

The photo below of the Great Theater of Ephesus is possibly of the Roman theater which dated a little later than Paul's time. It was however in Paul's time already a major theater and gathering place of the citizens of Ephesus. In Ephesus there was also another minor theater, a magnificent agora, and a school (hall) of Tyrannus which we read of in Acts 19:8 ff where Paul taught for three months. The hall of Tyrannus is believed to be across the street from the great theater of Ephesus.

We read of the Goddess Artemis and Paul's encounter with Demetrius the silver smith in Acts 19:23ff:

> *"About that time there arose no little stir concerning the Way. [24] For a man named Demetrius, a silversmith, who made silver shrines of Artemis, brought no little business to the craftsmen. [25] These he gathered together, with the workmen of like occupation, and said, "Men, you know that from this business we have our wealth. [26] And you*

*see and hear that not only at Ephesus but almost
throughout all Asia this Paul has persuaded and turned
away a considerable company of people, saying that
Gods made with hands are not Gods. [27]And there is
danger not only that this trade of ours may come into
disrepute but also that the temple of the great Goddess
Artemis may count for nothing, and that she may even be
deposed from her magnificence, she whom all Asia and
the world worship." [28]When they heard this they were
enraged, and cried out, "Great is Artemis of the
Ephesians!" [29]So the city was filled with the confusion;
and they rushed together into the theater, dragging with
them Gaius and Aristarchus, Macedonians who were
Paul's companions in travel. [30]Paul wished to go in
among the crowd, but the disciples would not let him;
[31]some of the Asiarchs also, who were friends of his, sent
to him and begged him not to venture into the
theater. [32]Now some cried one thing, some another; for
the assembly was in confusion, and most of them did not
know why they had come together. [33]Some of the crowd
prompted Alexander, whom the Jews had put forward.
And Alexander motioned with his hand, wishing to make
a defense to the people. [34]But when they recognized that
he was a Jew, for about two hours they all with one voice
cried out, "Great is Artemis of the Ephesians!" [35]And
when the town clerk had quieted the crowd, he said,
"Men of Ephesus, what man is there who does not know
that the city of the Ephesians is temple keeper of the great
Artemis, and of the sacred stone that fell from the
sky? [36]Seeing then that these things cannot be
contradicted, you ought to be quiet and do nothing
rash. [37]For you have brought these men here who are
neither sacrilegious nor blasphemers of our Goddess. [38]If
therefore Demetrius and the craftsmen with him have a
complaint against any one, the courts are open, and there
are proconsuls; let them bring charges against one*

another. [39]But if you seek anything further, it shall be settled in the regular assembly. [40]For we are in danger of being charged with rioting today, there being no cause that we can give to justify this commotion." [41]And when he had said this, he dismissed the assembly."

The Church in Ephesus

We are uncertain as to who actually founded the church in Ephesus. We read of Paul's work in Ephesus in Acts 18:18-20:1. Acts 18:18-19:7:

> *"After this Paul stayed many days longer, and then took leave of the brethren and sailed for Syria, and with him Priscilla and Aquila. At Cenchreae he cut his hair, for he had a vow. [19]And they came to Ephesus, and he left them there; but he himself went into the synagogue and argued with the Jews. [20]When they asked him to stay for a longer period, he declined; [21]but on taking leave of them he said, "I will return to you if God wills," and he set sail from Ephesus. [22]When he had landed at Caesarea, he went up and greeted the church, and then went down to Antioch. [23]After spending some time there he departed and went from place to place through the region of Galatia and Phrygia, strengthening all the disciples. [24]Now a Jew named Apollos, a native of Alexandria, came to Ephesus. He was an eloquent man, well versed in the scriptures. [25]He had been instructed in the way of the Lord; and being fervent in spirit, he spoke and taught accurately the things concerning Jesus, though he knew only the baptism of John. [26]He began to speak boldly in the synagogue; but when Priscilla and Aquila heard him, they took him and expounded to him the way of God more accurately. [27]And when he wished to cross to Achaia, the brethren encouraged him, and wrote to the disciples to receive him. When he arrived, he greatly helped those who through grace had believed, [28]for he powerfully confuted the Jews in public, showing*

by the scriptures that the Christ was Jesus.
[19:1]While Apollos was at Corinth, Paul passed through the upper country and came to Ephesus. There he found some disciples. [2]And he said to them, "Did you receive the Holy Spirit when you believed?" And they said, "No, we have never even heard that there is a Holy Spirit." [3]And he said, "Into what then were you baptized?" They said, "Into John's baptism." [4]And Paul said, "John baptized with the baptism of repentance, telling the people to believe in the one who was to come after him, that is, Jesus." [5]On hearing this, they were baptized in the name of the Lord Jesus. [6]And when Paul had laid his hands upon them, the Holy Spirit came on them; and they spoke with tongues and prophesied. [7]There were about twelve of them in all. [8]And he entered the synagogue and for three months spoke boldly, arguing and pleading about the kingdom of God; [9]but when some were stubborn and disbelieved, speaking evil of the Way before the congregation, he withdrew from them, taking the disciples with him, and argued daily in the hall of Tyrannus. [10]This continued for two years, so that all the residents of Asia heard the word of the Lord, both Jews and Greeks."

When Paul left Corinth on his second missionary journey he spent a short while in Ephesus, leaving Priscilla and Aquila in Ephesus. He travelled on to Caesarea, Galatia, and Phrygia, then returned to Ephesus where Priscilla and Aquila had converted an eloquent Jew named Apollos. Apollos returned to Corinth leaving Priscilla and Aquila in Ephesus. In Ephesus Paul found a number of disciples who had been baptized into John the Baptist's baptism. Acts 19:1 ff records that Paul taught them about Christian baptism and baptized them into Christ.

Paul taught in the synagogue for three months and then remained in Ephesus for two years. While in Ephesus his ministry reached into all Asia (the Roman province of Asia, now

Turkey.) At Acts 19:10 Luke records that while Paul was in Ephesus all the residents of Asia heard the word of the Lord.

This would have been around A.D. 53.

During the last half of the 1st century A.D three prominent Christian evangelists were associated with Ephesus and that region of Asia; the Apostle Paul, Timothy, and the Apostle John.

The church in Ephesus became the most prominent and influential church in the Roman Province of Asia and towards the close of the first century possibly the most influential church in Christendom.

Major Lessons to Learn from this Study

- Where was the Roman Province of Asia located? In what modern country would it be located today?
- Why was the city of Ephesus so important to the Roman Province of Asia?
- What three features of Ephesus dominated city life?
- Who was Artemis and why was she important to Ephesus?
- What do we learn about Demetrius?

Discussion Questions

- Why would the church in Ephesus have been so important to Paul's ministry in Asia and to the religious makeup of churches in Asia?
- How important has Ephesus been to church life through the centuries of church history? Consider three important evangelists in Ephesus and their role and place in our New Testament.
- How many New Testament books involve the church in and around Ephesus? Include John's Gospel and Epistles, Paul's Epistles, and Revelation.

Lesson 3

Introduction to the Primary Theology of Ephesians

It is extremely important to know the primary theological emphases of Ephesians since all the major points in the epistle develop these themes or are related to them in some form.

First, we will shortly demonstrate from within text that the primary theology or message of Ephesians is that Christians are predestined by God to so live that they bring glory to God in Christ Jesus and the church.

Notice how Paul develops this central theology in the *Laudatio* (prayer and praise section) of Ephesians.

> *"Blessed be the God and Father of our Lord Jesus Christ, who has blessed us in Christ with every spiritual blessing in the heavenly places. [4] even as he chose us in him before the foundation of the world, that we should be holy and blameless before him. [5] He destined us in love to be his sons through Jesus Christ, according to the purpose of his will, [6] to the praise of his glorious grace which he freely bestowed on us in the Beloved. [7] In him we have redemption through his blood, the forgiveness of our trespasses, according to the riches of his grace [8] which he lavished upon us. [9] For he has made known to us in all wisdom and insight the mystery of his will, according to his purpose which he set forth in Christ [10] as a plan for the fulness of time, to unite all things in him, things in heaven and things on earth. [11] In him, according to the purpose of him who accomplishes all things according to the counsel of his will, [12] we who first hoped in Christ have been destined and appointed to live for the praise of his glory. [13] In him you also, who have heard the word of truth, the gospel of your salvation, and have believed in him, were sealed with the promised Holy*

Spirit, [14] which is the guarantee of our inheritance until we acquire possession of it, to the praise of his glory."[3]

Paul affirms that according to God's eternal purpose and plan God has *called* and *destined* Christians corporately[4] to be his children *in Christ Jesus.* The technical theological term for this eternal plan is *Heilsgeschichte,* a German word that states that God has worked out his eternal purpose of redemption in history, which is in the history of Israel, Jesus Christ, and the church.

Paul continues to assert that Christians *in Christ* are *destined[5]* according to God's plan and purpose to *so live their lives that they bring glory to God,* cf. Eph 1:5, 9 and 10.

This translates into both *doctrinal-theological* and *paranetic* (practical, ethical) concerns regarding why and how we should live, cf Eph 4:1 ff.

As he works through Ephesians Paul uses an interesting expression to draw attention to the central issue. He uses this expression strategically three times, "*For this reason …*" cf. Eph 1:15; 3:1; 3:14. Thus, "*for this reason, that we are destined to so live that we bring glory to God in Christ and the church,* we should live lives that are different from our secular or pagan neighbors. What Paul means by this is that it is our calling as Christians to so live as Christians in Christ and the church *that we will bring glory to God.*

Central to this purpose of living according to our calling to bring glory to God is the need for Christians *to constantly and earnestly maintain the unity of the Spirit in the bond of peace,* cf.

---

[3] I have italicized certain expressions for emphasis.

[4] By corporately we have in mind the church as a body of people, not focusing on the individual. We are corporately in Christ called to be saved and bring glory to God. We will develop this distinction below in an excursus on Calvinistic versus Pauline predestination. You will find this excursus in Lesson 5a (see Table of Contents)

[5] The expression *destined* from προορίζω, *proorízō,* which means *decided before,* is the same as *predestined.* We will learn in a later lesson that this does not refer to Calvinistic Predestination. Biblical predestination is based on God's foreknowledge, grace and our choice to believe and not on God's arbitrary choice of who will be saved and who not.

Eph 4:1-3. A divided church cannot reflect the glory of God! Primarily in the Ephesian situation this involved Jews and Gentiles living together in peace and harmony in the church. By application today this means that Christians should be eager to maintain the unity of the body of Christ, the church, and get along with one another even though we might differ in some doctrinal issues. Cf. Rom 14:1-23.

A *secondary theological message* of Ephesians is the emphasis on what God has done for us out of his love and grace *in and through Jesus Christ*! By God's gracious giving of his son Jesus Christ *to die for all*, both Jew and Gentile are saved in the one body of Christ. Furthermore it is through Jesus' faithfulness to God's purpose and calling, and our faith in God's working in Jesus that both Jews and Gentiles can be saved and restored to a right relationship with God through faith (trusting) in Jesus Christ. The theme "for by grace you are saved through faith in Jesus Christ", Eph 2:8, is a significant theological theme in Ephesians.

Christ, and being in Christ, and God working through Christ, dominates Paul's thinking in Ephesians. Note how many times this emphasis of *in Christ, in him, through him*, etc. is made in the *Laudatio*, Eph 1:2-14; at least 10 times! In the whole epistle *Christ* appears 46 times in 43 verses. The expressions being "*in Christ*", "*in him*", "*with him*", *through him*", etc. occur at least 30 times in Ephesians. It is not by accident that this theme of *in Christ* or *through Christ* dominates this *Laudatio*, the first block of theological material in the epistle, and also the whole epistle.

Third, Paul explains that the cosmic scope of God's work in Christ is centered in Christ's death and resurrection. The death of Christ has impact not only on earth but also on the heavenly or spiritual places. The death of Christ brought about the reconciliation of all men to God. The death of Christ brought about the reconciliation of Jew and Gentile in one body. In Jesus' death and resurrection God defeated Satan and the spiritual powers that are believed to control our destiny. In Christ, Christians through the death and resurrection of Jesus also decisively defeat all spiritual powers and demons, cf. Eph 1:22, 6:12; Col 1:13. Through the cross Christ has supremacy over all things (powers) *for the church.*

Thus the purpose of the church is to bring glory to God through Jesus Christ and in the church by demonstrating what God has done in Christ through his death and resurrection. How the Christian's lives have been shaped by the cross and the Holy Spirit brings glory to God and his eternal purpose. How Christians walk by the Spirit and not by the flesh demonstrates the power of God transforming their lives!

The central doctrinal/theological emphasis of Ephesians is that in Christ and the church Christians have been destined by God to bring glory to God in the one body[6] of Christ.

Another related theological emphasis related to the first is that God has done all this in and through Jesus Christ and he has done this *for all people, both Jew and Gentile.* To experience God's blessings and victory over all spiritual powers both Jew and Gentile together must live peaceably in Christ, or in his body the church.

The *paranetic*[7] (practical) emphasis of Ephesians resulting out of and relating to the theological centers of the epistle is that Christians must live good moral lives in their worldly communities in order to demonstrate and bring glory to God in Christ and the church. By living immoral lives in their communities Christians cannot bring glory to God.

Major *paranetic* themes to the central theological emphases in Ephesians are that Christians must *maintain the unity of the Spirit in the bond of peace* and *live moral and family lives* in keeping with the glory of God, Eph 4:1 ff. Through the cross and the work of the Holy Spirit both Jews and Gentiles have been brought into *one body.* Both Jewish and Gentile Christians

---

[6] Paul uses the sense of the body of Christ corporately to refer the church that Christ died to establish, cf. Matt 16:16-18; Eph 1;22, 23, Col 1:18.

[7] The term *paranetic* is a technical term referring to the practical ethical life Christians must live as the extension in their predestined divine calling in Christ.

will need to make every effort empowered by the indwelling Holy Spirit in order to do this. By maintaining the unity of the body of Christ, the church demonstrates the working (manifold working) of God through Christ and the Spirit.

Major Lessons to Learn from this Study

- The primary theology and message of Ephesians is that Christians are called to so live that they bring glory to God in Christ and the church.
- A secondary theological emphasis is that God has called and destined all people, both Jew and Gentile, *in and through Christ* to be saved.
- Paul stresses that God has a purpose and plan (*Heilsgeschichte*, plan of salvation) that he has been working since before the foundation of the earth.
- Note how many times *in Christ* or *in him* or *through him* appear in the epistle.
- The activity and work of the Holy Spirit is very important to God's work in and for his people.

Discussion Questions

- What two major emphases should be the center of our theology? How does the church play into this?
- How do these theological emphases impact our worship, ministry, and personal life in general?
- How does the death and resurrection play a cosmic role in our affairs?
- Discuss how this cosmic dimension of Christ's death can impact our everyday lives?
- How does our personal faith, commitment, and corporate ministry bring glory to God in practice?

Lesson 4

Certain Interesting Characteristics of Ephesians

What distinguishes Ephesians from the other Pauline epistles is that it was most likely intended to be a circular letter to several churches. The address of the Epistle to the Ephesians is somewhat unique! The address "to the *saints who are also (indeed) faithful in Christ Jesus*" which most likely omits a geographical location such as "who are at Ephesus" or "which is at Corinth" in Paul's epistles is notable. Likewise the lack of a personal greeting as in Paul's Pastoral Epistles "to Timothy" is also somewhat distinctive.

Thus it appears that Ephesians might have first been sent to Ephesus, intended as a circular epistle, then copied and sent on to other churches in Asia. We will comment more on this in our study of the text in our next lesson.

As a circular letter it does not discuss the concerns of only one local congregation's problems and issues, but is more general covering several factors that would impact Christians elsewhere in Asia. The issues that are discussed are therefore "universal" to all churches area of Asia, and even for churches and Christians today.

In Ephesians we have weighty statements of God's work both in the physical world and the cosmic world of spiritual powers.

Luke Timothy Johnson observes that prayer is a "pervasive atmosphere" and "most distinctive feature" of the epistle. Cf. Eph 2:14ff.

The Holy Spirit is also a prominent emphasis in Ephesians: Cf. Eph 1:13; 3:14-21; 4:1-3.

In fact the epistle touches on all of the major Pauline theological emphases; justification by grace through faith in Jesus cf. Eph 2:1-10; the redemptive power of the cross, cf. Eph 2:16; the transforming power of the Holy Spirit, cf. Eph 3:16ff; the gift of the Holy Spirit in empowering Christians and building up their faith, cf. Eph 3:16ff; Paul's concern for the relationship of the Jews and Gentiles, and God's plan to unite them in one body by the cross, cf. Eph 2:12-22; the importance of Christians living good moral lives as they impact their pagan neighbors, Eph 4:17 ff; the need for Christians to observe high family standards out of reverence for Christ, Eph 5:21 ff; and the spiritual war conducted by Satan and his demonic agents against the church and Christians, cf Eph 6:10 ff.

Paul explains that it was his conviction that it was his and the church's God given ministry to proclaim "good news". Paul explains that he had received this ministry and message as a revelation from God. Furthermore, his message was intended for all people, both Jew and Gentile.

How God would unite Jew and Gentile in peace had been a mystery for ages, even to Paul, but the message of how the Jew and Gentile were to be reconciled in one body was revealed to Paul as the work of God in Jesus through the death of Jesus on the cross, cf. Eph 3:1ff. In fact Paul believed that in Christ, in the fullness of time, God will reconcile all creation to himself. Cf. Eph 1:10.

The Cultural and Religious World of Ephesus and Asia

We have already mentioned the *Artemesian cult* and mystery religions in Ephesus, notably related to the temple of Artemis. The temple and Artemis' cult with its pagan and immoral practices seemingly dominated the city and culture of Ephesus. Cf. Acts 19:23 ff.

In the classical period of Greek mythology, dating as early as Homer (ca 750 BC), Artemis was described as the daughter of Zeus and Leto, and the twin sister of Apollo. She was the Greek and Arcadian goddess of the hunt, wild animals, the wilderness, childbirth, virginity, fertility, the protector of young girls, and the one responsible for relieving disease in women; she often was also depicted as a huntress carrying a bow and arrows.

It was primarily because of the immorality associated with the fertility cult associated with the goddess Artemis that Christianity had problems with the Artemesian cult. The fertility cult which included sexual immorality was a major aspect and religious practice in Ephesus. Cf. Eph 5:1ff. We know from archeological discoveries of the presence of a major brothel on the main street on the road from the harbor to the center of the city.

The ancient mystery religions were also a major feature of Ephesian and Asian religious practice. Mystery religions were concerned with esoteric means including drunkenness which was assumed to introduce one to a special relationship with divine and spiritual powers. Through trances induced by a variety of means and practices the individual could escape the confines of the physical world, enter the spiritual world, and gain access to the divine.

Gnosticism, although only in its early form, which is known in scholarly circles as incipient Gnosticism, or early undeveloped forms of Gnosticism, was becoming a major feature of Asian philosophical and religious practices. *Gnosis* is the Greek word for *knowledge*. Gnosticism was a philosophical view that stressed possession of a *special form of intuitive knowledge* that was considered necessary for overcoming the spiritual powers that surrounded the physical and cosmic realms surrounding the life of the individual.

Without this special knowledge which was not learned but which one received by special spiritual endowment one could not escape from the powers of the spiritual world.

Gnosticism was a form of Platonism which held that the physical world was evil and not permanent. In contrast with the physical world the spiritual world was permanent and pure. By special *intuitive* knowledge (*gnosis*) one was enabled to escape the physical world and those spiritual powers (known as *demiurges,* sometimes *demigods*) that reigned over the physical world.

This mood was already by the 60s A.D. becoming a problem faced by Christians. In the 2nd century A.D. Gnosticism became a major divisive threat to Christianity.

To get a sense of the Gnostic mindset refer to the chart below that diagrams the Gnostic cosmology. Cosmology refers to the discussion of the cosmos including the physical world; how it originated and is controlled. We might today speak of the universe, how it came into being and how it is controlled. Gnosticism argued that a physical world which is essentially evil and transitory could not have been created by a good loving god since according to the Platonic world view the physical world is for all intents and purposes evil.

The Gnostic view was that a renegade disobedient son of the ultimate good god had placed in the physical world an evil spirit which corrupted everything that touched it. Therefore if Jehovah (*Ialdoboth* in their terminology) created everything physical he could not be a pure good god full of light. Full blown Gnosticism of the 2nd century A.D. rejected Judaism and everything Jewish, notably the Old Testament since it proclaimed a message regarding Jehovah who in the Gnostic minds was an inferior God. This however was more of a later 2nd century challenge to the Christians but the root of this heresy was developing at the time of Paul and his ministry.

The Christian answer to Gnosticism was that the eternally good God, Jehovah, is the pure light who created everything. Jesus, Jehovah's son, claimed to be the light that came into the world (John 8:5; 9:5) and Christians argued that everything the Gnostics were looking for was found in Jesus. In fact, it was in Jesus, the light of the world, that Christians argued they were enlightened and found their way to God. When Thomas asked where Jesus was going when he spoke of leaving them Jesus answered, cf. John 14:5, 6:

> *"5 Thomas said to him, "Lord, we do not know where you are going; how can we know the way?" 6 Jesus said to him, "I am the way, and the truth, and the life; no one comes to the Father, but by me. 7 If you had known me, you would have known my Father also; henceforth you know him and have seen him."*

The Christian response to Gnosticism and the evil in the world was that it was Satan who had entered in and corrupted the world and Jesus the son of the pure God had come to save the world. Christians argued that Jesus in his death and resurrection had conquered Satan and the spiritual powers and had provided all one needed for true spiritual and eternal life. This is a major point that Paul argues in both Ephesians and Colossians.

Some Gnostic Concepts

- The real God is Pure Light, Pure Spirit, and not Jehovah!
- The Pure God could not have created a corrupt world.
- Lesser god's exist who are not Pure Light but who are descendants of the Pure God who had fallen from the Pure Light.
- "*Ialdoboth*" was a son of the Pure God who rebelled against the Pure God. *Ialdoboth* is considered to be Jehovah!
- "*Ialdoboth*" was the impure god who created the evil physical world.
- Gnosis is Knowledge, but a special esoteric knowledge attainable by only the select.
- Man needs pure spiritual esoteric knowledge which is not the normal human knowledge of this world.
- Man needs this special intuitive knowledge to escape the powers of this world.
- This is special intuitive knowledge that comes directly from the Pure God of Light.
- This knowledge reveals the Pure Light necessary to escape the evil powers.
- Mysticism involves such special intuitive knowledge.
- Mysticism involves a secret working of a Redeemer of Light.
- A "Gnostic Redeemer" provides this secret knowledge.
- Spiritual powers pervade and control the cosmos.
- They are the Principalities and Powers.

- They roam the Heavenly Places.
- Man needs this special intuitive knowledge to escape from the Spiritual powers (Demiurges).
- *Stoicheion* – is a technical term used to describe these special elemental powers of the universe.

Gnostic Cosmology

- Gnostic cosmology is a way of looking at the universe.
- It has a strong neo-Platonic world view which sees the physical creation as corrupt and decaying.
- The spiritual world is the real world, not this physical world we live in.
- The body is evil, the spirit is pure.
- The spirit is held captive in the physical body and desires release (salvation).
- The god that created the corrupt world is evil.
- The real God is pure light and spirit and is beyond human contact.
- The spirit of man seeks to escape the physical world and have communion with the ultimate good God of light.
- The world is surrounded by concentric rings of demigods or demiurges who keep man in the physical world and away from the real God. They are sometimes referred to as the "principalities and powers in the heavenly places".
- The ultimate god of pure light sends a "spiritual leader" into the world who guides the spirit back to him through pure *gnosis* knowledge.
- The way back to the pure god is through the correct kind of "intuitive" knowledge, hence the term Gnostic from gnosis meaning knowledge.

- Refer to the Gnostic Cosmology diagram below.

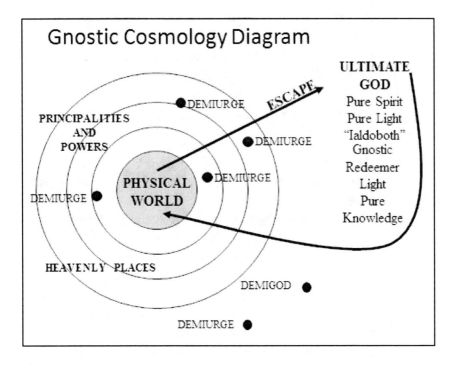

Major Lessons to Learn from this Study

- Note the flow of thought in the epistle; first theology, then practical paranetic living based on the theological emphases.
- Note the role of the Holy Spirit and prayer in the epistle. Eph 3:14ff.
- Be able to discuss the cultural and religious nature of Ephesus.
- Be able to discuss Gnosticism, the *stoicheia*, and the principalities in heavenly places and their role in Ephesians.

Discussion Questions

- How do we understand the central concern of Ephesians which is God's *corporate* calling for Christians to be children *in Christ*? What does this *corporate* emphasis mean?
- What role does the Holy Spirit play in the Christian's life? Cf. Eph 1:14; Eph 3:14-21; and Eph 4:1-3.
- We may not be subject to Gnostic powers today, but how can Gnosticism or a form of Gnosticism and mysterious spiritual powers impact our lives today? Remember that Gnosticism is an emphasis on *knowledge* as the means of salvation or deliverance in religion. Are we saved today by how much knowledge we have or the right kind of knowledge? Be careful! Are we saved by our knowledge or by God's grace?
- What role should knowledge play in salvation? What should its focus be?
- What should be the center of our faith?
- What kind of spiritual powers take over our lives today? What is the solution to this? Cf. Eph 3:14-21.

Lesson 5

Ephesians 1:1-14
The Prescript, Salutation, and *Laudatio*
in Paul's Epistemology

*¹ Paul, an apostle of Christ Jesus by the will of God,
To the saints who are also faithful in Christ Jesus:
² Grace to you and peace from God our Father and the
Lord Jesus Christ.
³ Blessed be the God and Father of our Lord Jesus
Christ, who has blessed us in Christ with every spiritual
blessing in the heavenly places, ⁴ even as he chose us in
him before the foundation of the world, that we should be
holy and blameless before him. ⁵ He destined us in love to
be his sons through Jesus Christ, according to the
purpose of his will, ⁶ to the praise of his glorious grace
which he freely bestowed on us in the Beloved. ⁷ In him
we have redemption through his blood, the forgiveness of
our trespasses, according to the riches of his grace
⁸ which he lavished upon us. ⁹ For he has made known to
us in all wisdom and insight the mystery of his will,
according to his purpose which he set forth in Christ ¹⁰ as
a plan for the fulness of time, to unite all things in him,
things in heaven and things on earth.
¹¹ In him, according to the purpose of him who
accomplishes all things according to the counsel of his
will, ¹² we who first hoped in Christ have been destined
and appointed to live for the praise of his glory. ¹³ In him
you also, who have heard the word of truth, the gospel of
your salvation, and have believed in him, were sealed
with the promised Holy Spirit, ¹⁴ which is the guarantee
of our inheritance until we acquire possession of it, to the
praise of his glory."*

Understanding the structure of a Pauline epistle or any epistle
is vital to interpretation of the epistle. For example, we can

partially determine the origin of a letter today merely by examining the date! 12.31.2013 as against 31.12.2013. Which one is American and which is British or European?

Early in his ministry Paul adapted the typical Graeco/Roman form of letter writing into an early Christian Epistolary instructional and exhortative form. This standard Pauline form of letter writing was structured around four major components, *Prescript, Laudatio, Body, and Conclusion.*[8] These are described as follows:

A *Prescript* which includes a greeting, and salutation in which Paul would describe to whom he was writing and include some form of greeting.

A *Laudatio* (a praise and prayer section). This section is very important to determining the theology and purpose of the epistle because in this material Paul introduces his purpose and major theme of the epistle. The *Laudatio* would generally be in the form of, or include a major prayer for the recipients.

The *Body* of the letter which often came in two sections:

Doctrine/Theology – which outlines and develops Paul's major premise and argument.

Paranesis – in which Paul would introduce the practical or ethical implications of the doctrinal material.

The *Conclusion* in which Paul summarizes his main purpose in writing and mentions friends with whom the recipients of the letter would be acquainted.

Enlarged Structural Outline of the Ephesian Epistle

Prescript, Greeting, and Salutation - 1:1-2; greetings and Salutation.

Laudatio - 1:3-23 (praise and prayer section) in which Paul introduces his major theological theme and prays for the church.

Body of the Letter - 2:1-6:20 which normally would be in two sections.

---

[8] Some scholars use different yet similar terms to describe these elements of an ancient epistle.

The *Doctrine/Theology* material; 2:1-3:21 where Paul
introduces the theology upon which he builds his
practical or paranetic material.

Paranesis; 4:1-6:20 where Paul discusses the practical
teaching material arising from the doctrinal material.

Conclusion; 6:21-24 where Paul usually would include
personal greetings.

The Prescript, Greeting, and Salutation - Eph 1:1-2

Eph 1:1. *"Paul, an apostle of Christ Jesus by the will of
God"*. Paul was an apostle *by the will of God* not by the will of
men or by his own will. Paul makes this comment because some
challenged the source of his apostleship and charged that his
authority was different from that of the other apostles. Here as in
Colossians and Galatians (as elsewhere) Paul stressed that his
apostleship and authority were not passed on to him by men, but
came directly from God. Cf. Gal 1:1. The stress on his divinely
pointed apostleship focused attention on the divine authority of
his message.

"To the saints who are also faithful in Christ Jesus:" Here we
encounter the ellipsis in which some manuscripts do not include
in Ephesus while other manuscripts read *"in Ephesus"*. As I will
mention in the following paragraphs, some of the better
manuscripts leave *in Ephesus* out considering Ephesians to be a
circular epistle to several churches in Asia.

The RSV does not include the locality *in Ephesus*. The
Aland United Bible Society Greek text (UBS) places [*en Ephesō*]
which reads *in Ephesus* between square parentheses [ ] indicating
manuscript issues. The United Bible Society, Kurt Aland et al,
1968 Greek text ranks the inclusion *in Ephesus* at a C indicating
that the evidence is not strong for including *in Ephesus*.

The NIV reads *"To the saints in Ephesus, [a] the faithful in
Christ Jesus"*. The footnote [a] following *Ephesus* in the NIV
indicates that some manuscripts do not include *in Ephesus*.

The manuscript testimony for including *in Ephesus* is not as
strong as some of the major manuscripts which omit the

expression. Those omitting it are P[46] (ca 200 AD), X (Sinaiticus ca 4th cent), B (Vaticanus ca 4th cent), Basil, Origen. Including the expression *in Ephesus* as mentioned above is ranked C in the UBS Greek text, 4th ed., of 2001. The 1979 26th edition of the Nestle-Aland Greek Text agrees with the UBS Greek text, questioning the strength of the inclusion of *in Ephesus*. Bruce Metzger, *A Textual Commentary on the Greek New Testament*, 1994 agrees with the UBS and Nestle-Aland Texts, questioning the "authenticity" of the inclusion in the expression *in Ephesus*.[9]

Eph 1:2. "*Grace and peace from God the Father and the Lord Jesus Christ*" is a typical Pauline, Christian greeting. It is believed by some scholars to be an original Pauline expression and it was Paul who had Christianized the traditional Greek epistolary greeting.

"*Grace*" *derives* from the Greek χάρις, *cháris* meaning *favor*. Sometimes we define this as unmerited favor, which it certainly is, but the word simply means *favor*. In giving his son to die on the cross God did all mankind a favor which we did not deserve and for which we could not pay nor work for, thus the gift of Jesus was an unmerited gift of God's grace.

"*Peace*" derives from the Greek εἰρήνη, *eirēnē* and like the Hebrew greeting *Shalom* refers to *inner spiritual peace and blessing*.

In Pauline theology Christians are *saved by God's grace through their faith in Jesus*. Christians do not deserve such a gift of salvation and cannot work enough to deserve it. *Salvation* is a gift of God's *grace* (favor). Cf. Eph 2:8, 9. It is a fundamental principle of Pauline and biblical theology that salvation is a gift of God's grace and is not received because we have earned it by works, no matter what kind of works we may offer. Christians are thus justified and saved by God's grace through their faith in

---

[9] For scholarly discussion of this cf. Andrew Lincoln, *Ephesians*, Word Biblical Commentary, p. 1, Notes; Clinton Arnold, *Exegetical Commentary on the New Testament*, Introduction; Robert Gundry, *Commentary on Ephesians*, Ephesians 1:1, 2; Peter O'Brian, *The Letter to the Ephesians*, Eph 1:1, 2.

Jesus. Only in this way can Christians then have peace with God. Note Paul's comments on this in two major texts in his Epistle to the Romans. Rom 3:21, 22:

> *"But now the righteousness of God has been manifested apart from law, although the law and the prophets bear witness to it.* [22] *the righteousness of God through faith in Jesus Christ for all who believe. For there is no distinction:* [23] *since all have sinned and fall short of the glory of God.* [24] *they are justified by his grace as a gift, through the redemption which is in Christ Jesus..."*

Rom 5:1, 2 adds the thought that it is only in this manner that Christians can have peace with God:

> *"Therefore, since we are justified by faith, we have peace with God through our Lord Jesus Christ.* [2] *Through him we have obtained access to this grace in which we stand, and we rejoice in our hope of sharing the glory of God ..."*

The Laudatio – Eph 1:3-14

The *Laudatio* is a literary introductory device common to many ancient Graeco/Roman epistles. Paul developed this *Laudatio* principle into a major Christian epistolary form. With the exception of Galatians we find a *Laudatio* in all of Paul's epistles. In the *Laudatio* Paul prays for the recipients and introduces his major theological theme.

Laudatio simply means *praise*, hence the *Laudatio* section in Paul's epistles is where he *praises God* and the recipients of the epistle. In the *Laudatio* Paul also introduces the theology of the something that this must be forefront in his mind!

We have already noted in the introduction to this epistle that the central theological theme of Ephesians is that *Christians should so live that they bring glory to God through Christ and the church*. This theme is spelled out in the *Laudatio*.

In this *Laudatio* section we also find one of the other major ingredients of Paul's theological program. *God works according to his own eternal predetermined plan!*

Christians are saved by God's grace through the faithfulness of Jesus and the faith of the believer in God's working in Jesus. This salvation was all *according to a plan God determined before the foundation of the world.*

As noted above in technical terms we call this redemptive plan of salvation *Heilsgeschichte*, that is a salvation plan *worked out in history.* God has worked his plan in history through humans such as Abraham and Moses, finally through Jesus, in real time history, to bring about his redemption of mankind. This is an important concept to emphasize since the Gnostics held that salvation and redemption came through special non historical intuitive knowledge rather than in the historical fact of Jesus' death and resurrection. Paul argues that it was through the death and resurrection of Jesus that redemption and salvation are found, not in any kind of special esoteric knowledge. Cf. 1 Cor 15:1-4:

> "Now I would remind you, brethren, in what terms I preached to you the gospel, which you received, in which you stand, [2] by which you are saved, if you hold it fast—unless you believed in vain. [3] For I delivered to you as of first importance what I also received, that Christ died for our sins in accordance with the scriptures, [4] that he was buried, that he was raised on the third day in accordance with the scriptures ..."

That God has called all to be his children according to an eternal plan is perhaps one of the most significant thoughts in Paul's epistle to the Ephesians since it explains *God's eternal purpose in Christ* for the church and explains in advance what shapes the remainder of the letter. *We have been destined since eternity to live for the glory of God* in Christ and in the church.

In this paragraph Paul discusses what he describes as the *pre-ordained* plan of God. God according to his *foreknowledge* had planned (*predestined* or *ordained, prooridzō*), even *before the foundation of the world,* that both Jews and Gentiles would be his children in Christ and that by living together as one body both Jews and Gentiles together would bring glory to God. On

Paul regarding the foreknowledge and predestination of God cf. also Rom 8:29-30. On the unity of believers, both Jew and Gentile in Christ, cf. Eph 4:1-7 which we will discuss in due course.

In Ephesians 2 Paul develops an enlargement of this theme of both Jew and Gentile being saved in one body by the cross. It is a major theme in Ephesians that both Jew and Gentile must realize that they are saved only by grace of God through faith in Jesus and by the working of God in Christ. This was the plan preordained by God in Christ; hence Paul's observations regarding this in the *Laudatio*. Only by living together in unity in one body through the cross can the Jewish and Gentile Christians bring glory to God.

Thus in order to *bring glory to God* as his children *in Christ* the Jewish and Gentile Christians must learn to get along together in the *one body* of Christ, *which is the church.*

Paul will later introduce the theme that in order to do this Christians will need to be zealous and serious in this effort and furthermore will need the power of the indwelling Holy Spirit.

This introductory prayer and praise section thus sets the tone for the remainder of the epistle.

Eph 1:3. The term *"blessed"* (Greek εὐλογητός, *eulogḗtós*, Hebrew *berakah*) is a form of Jewish blessing *pronounced on God for his great mercy and redeeming action.* The NIV translates this *"Praise be to the God and Father..."* The Greek reads *eulogḗtós* for *blessed* which can be translated *worthy of praise* or *blessing.* In the New Testament *eulogḗtós* is used *only of God and Christ. Eulogḗtós* is similar to a related Greek word εὐλογία, *eulogía* which basically means *a good saying* and is the basis for our English word eulogy which often describes the *kind or good words* that are said of one at a funeral. *Eulogḗtós* emphasizes that Christians are to live *for the praise of His glory* and begin doing so by praising God for planning their salvation in Christ before the creation of the world and for calling all Christians to be His children in Christ. *Notice the emphasis on what God has done* for *all Christians* (his eternal purpose) *in*

Christ. The stress is not simply on the individual but on what God has done for them in Christ, corporately.

Eph 1:3. Paul praises God because God "has *blessed* us in Christ with every spiritual blessing in the heavenly places." The word *blessed* (*eulogēsas,* an aorist participle of εὐλογέω, *eulogéō*) indicates that God *has already blessed* Christians with every spiritual blessing they might need in the heavenly places (a loaded expression) or in the spiritual world.

There is nothing Christians need in their spiritual life that God has not already supplied or provided *in Christ Jesus.* This is an important point in view of the presence of Gnostic tendencies in Ephesus. Recall the Gnostic cosmology we noticed in our Introduction to Ephesians. Gnostics taught that Christians needed *special intuitive knowledge* to escape the demiurges or spiritual powers that controlled the "heavenly places" that surround the physical earth. Contrary to this Paul's argument in Ephesians, and Colossians, is that *in Christ* God has *already provided* all the knowledge and power Christians need to overcome demonic spiritual influences. The knowledge Paul stresses is the *knowledge of Christ and what God achieved in Christ's death and resurrection.* Christianity does not hold to some form of esoteric intuitive knowledge that comes to a few enlightened people but simply proclaims the knowledge of what God has done for all in Christ Jesus and his death and resurrection.

Eph 1:4. Paul adds *"even as he has chosen us ..."* Being chosen by God before the foundation of the world strengthens the security God has provided for all Christians as his children. *God* has chosen us in Christ!

Paul adds that there was also a purpose in God's calling; *"that we should be holy and blameless..."* Without being holy and blameless Christians cannot bring glory to God who himself is holy and blameless.

Paul will add to this as he progresses in his letter that Christian salvation and holiness is provided for *all Christians,* both Jew and Gentile, equally by grace through faith in Jesus

Christ. God has also provided the Holy Spirit to assist *all Christians* in their Christian living for the glory of God.

That we are *chosen in Christ* with the purpose that we might be holy and blameless is very important! It is *in Christ* that we become holy and blameless, not by special knowledge as was held by the false teaching of Gnosticism.

In Christ God has provided Christians with an *escape* from all spiritual powers, and he has provided them with the power to *overcome* the spiritual powers.

Eph 1:5. We are *destined* (προορίζω, *proorízō, destined* or *predestined*) in God's love to be his sons through Jesus Christ. The Greek word for *destined* is *proorízō* which as we have noticed means *predestined* or *decided beforehand.* God decided before the foundation of the world that *in Christ* Christians (both Jew and Gentiles) would be his sons/children.

This is not Calvinistic predestination[10] which is based on a view of inherited sin, man's total depravity, God's arbitrary choice as to who will be saved and who eternally lost and doomed, and a view of God's irresistible grace. What we find in Paul's concept of predestination is a predestination *based on God's foreknowledge, love, and purpose* (Cf. Rom 8:28-30). Biblical predestination does not preclude God's grace and man's accessing that grace through faith, a point Paul will stress in Eph 2:1-10.

Contrary to Calvinistic predestination man's salvation is not based on an arbitrary decision by God but on man's willingness to trust in God's grace through trusting what God has worked in the death and resurrection of Jesus.

In Calvinistic predestination man has no choice and makes no decision. God makes the choice and the Holy Spirit does the work. Man is arbitrarily chosen by God either to be eternally saved or doomed. Thus in Calvinism man's response to God's calling is not made by man through faith, but by God's arbitrary choice.

---

[10] For a more comprehensive discussion of Calvinistic and Biblical predestination cf. chapter 5a following lesson 12 of this study.

At the conclusion of this study you will find three excursus on Pauline and Calvinistic predestination, the origin and cycle of faith, and the maturing of saving faith. Lesson 5a, p. 129; Lesson 5b, p. 157; Lesson 5c, p. 159.

Pauline and Biblical predestination states that God has according to his foreknowledge predestined that Christians should corporately be his children *in Christ*. Paul's understanding of predestination is a predestination in which God decided before creation that *those in Christ* would be his children. This is what we call a corporate predestination; God predestined that those *in Christ or in the body of Christ* would be saved.

However, Paul's theology states that Christians as individuals respond to God by their decision of faith and are then baptized into the body of Christ; cf Gal 3:23-29:

> *"Now before faith came, we were confined under the law, kept under restraint until faith should be revealed.* [24] *So that the law was our custodian until Christ came, that we might be justified by faith.* [25] *But now that faith has come, we are no longer under a custodian;* [26] *for in Christ Jesus you are all sons of God, through faith.* [27] *For as many of you as were baptized into Christ have put on Christ.* [28] *There is neither Jew nor Greek, there is neither slave nor free, there is neither male nor female; for you are all one in Christ Jesus.* [29] *And if you are Christ's, then you are Abraham's offspring, heirs according to promise."*

We decide to react in faith to God's gracious work in Christ and God's gracious calling. This response is not an arbitrary predestination but a free will response to God's calling. Cf. Eph 2:1-9, which we will shortly study in some detail:

Eph 1:5. This decision that we should be God's sons/children through Jesus Christ was according to God's predetermined will, not by accident or our working.

Eph 1:6. God is to be praised for his great and glorious mercy which he has freely bestowed on us *in the Beloved* (Jesus Christ):

"He destined us in love to be his sons through Jesus Christ, according to the purpose of his will, [6] to the praise of his glorious grace which he freely bestowed on us in the Beloved."

Eph 1:7. *In Christ* we *"have redemption through his blood and the forgiveness of our trespasses* according to the richness of his mercy. Thus *in Christ* through his blood as an act of God's rich grace he has lavishly provided *redemption* for us *in Christ.*

Redemption derives from the Greek ἀπολύτρωσις, *apolútrōsis* which means *deliverance, liberation, release, being set free.* We are set free *in Christ* from the bond of sin that binds us.

Forgiveness is from the Greek ἄφεσις, *áphesis* and means *cancellation of guilt, pardon, deliverance from guilt.*

The use of the present tense verb ἔχομεν, *echomen,* "we have" indicates that we *continually* and *constantly* have this deliverance in Christ.

Eph 1:8, 9. Paul explains that this gracious redemption God has richly *"lavished upon us. [9]For he has made known to us in all wisdom and insight the mystery of his will, according to his purpose which he set forth in Christ."*

The Greek is convoluted and actually reads something like this, "according to the abundance of his grace which he has lavished on us, in all wisdom and insight, he has made known the mystery of his will (or purpose or desire)".

The point is that God has *"abundantly made known to us in all wisdom and insight the mystery of his will."* What God has already done in Christ he has already clearly revealed to us? It was in the past a mystery how he would do this but now this mystery of how God would bless both Jew and Gentile according to his will and purpose *has been clearly revealed to us. We do not need any special intuitive knowledge to learn this.* We have this in the knowledge of what God has done for us in Christ.

Paul will return to this *mystery* on five other occasions in Ephesians, 3:3, 4, 9; 5:32; 6:19. *Mystery* (Greek μυστήριον, *mustērion, mystery or secret*) does not refer to something that cannot be known but to that which could be known but had not yet until Christ had been made known. The *mystery* was *how God was going to save both Jew and Gentile.* He was not going to do this through the Law of Moses (Cf. Galatians) for that would exclude the Gentiles. But now he has revealed that he has done this *in one body, the body of Christ, which is the church, by his grace though faith in Christ Jesus.*

The argument of both of Paul's epistles to the Galatians and Romans is that God does not have two plans, one for the Jews and another for the Gentiles. He has only one plan. His one plan is that Jews and Gentiles will all be saved in one body by the grace of God thorough faith for everyone in Christ Jesus.

Eph 1:9. We see God's eternal purpose explained and set forth *in Christ.* If you want to be a child of God and enjoy all God's provision for man, you must be *in Christ*! Gal 3:25-29 explains how one gets into Christ by faith in God and his working in Christ Jesus:

> *"But now that faith has come, we are no longer under a custodian;* [26] *for in Christ Jesus you are all sons of God, through faith.* [27] *For as many of you as were baptized into Christ have put on Christ.* [28] *There is neither Jew nor Greek, there is neither slave nor free, there is neither male nor female; for you are all one in Christ Jesus.* [29] *And if you are Christ's, then you are Abraham's offspring, heirs according to promise."*

Based on their faith in Christ Christians are all baptized into Christ and become one in Christ.

Eph 1:10. God's plan was an *eternal plan made before time* for *the fullness of time*:

> *"For he has made known to us in all wisdom and insight the mystery of his will, according to his purpose which he set forth in Christ* [10] *as a plan for the fulness of time, to unite all things in him, things in heaven and things on earth."*

Eph 1:11-14. This text explains God's plan, purpose, and will in greater detail:

"In him, according to the purpose of him who accomplishes all things according to the counsel of his will, [12] we who first hoped in Christ have been destined and appointed to live for the praise of his glory. [13] In him you also, who have heard the word of truth, the gospel of your salvation, and have believed in him, were sealed with the promised Holy Spirit, [14] which is the guarantee of our inheritance until we acquire possession of it, to the praise of his glory."

God is eminently capable of accomplishing what he plans. He has in fact already accomplished his purpose *in Christ according to his will and plan.*

Christians who have set their hope *in Christ* are *destined* (*prooridzō, predestined*) and *appointed to live for the praise of God's glory. Appointed*, Greek ἐκληρώθημεν, *eklērōthēmen*, derives from κληρόω, *klēróō* means *to cast lots, determine by lot, i.e., to determine something, choose someone.* Not only had God *predestined* us in Christ to be his children and to bring him glory in Christ and the church, he had *determined* that this should be! Cf our previous discussion of predestination or being destined at Eph 1:5.

Furthermore, *in Christ* we are *sealed by the Holy Spirit.* God has chosen to live in us through his Holy Spirit which he has given us as a *guarantee of our eternal inheritance.* The indwelling Holy Spirit is our sign of belonging to God and God dwelling in us. That God has given Christians the Holy Spirit to dwell in them, to assist them to live appropriately and to empower them, is a purely astonishing gift of God's grace. Thus God gives his Holy Spirit to man when through their faith and repentance man is baptized into Christ for the forgiveness of sins. Note Acts 2:38 and Acts 5:32:

Acts 2:38 "And Peter said to them, "Repent, and be baptized every one of you in the name of Jesus Christ for the forgiveness of your sins; and you shall receive the gift of the Holy Spirit" and Acts 5:32 "And we are witnesses to these things, and so is the Holy Spirit whom God has given to those who obey him."

At 1 Cor 12:12, 13 Paul builds on this concept of Christians receiving God's Hoy Spirit:

"For just as the body is one and has many members, and all the members of the body, though many, are one body, so it is with Christ. [13] For by one Spirit we were all baptized into one body—Jews or Greeks, slaves or free—and all were made to drink of one Spirit."

All of what God has done in Christ is *to the praise of God's glory*. This is an important key to understanding the theology of Ephesians. Note again that we are destined and appointed by God to live *for the praise of his glory* (1:12). What God has done in Christ is *for the praise of his glory* (1:14).

Notice how in the expression *"for this reason…"* Paul now picks up the theme of living for God's glory at 1:12 again in 1:15, *"For this reason…"* What reason? *That Christians should live for the praise of his glory*!

Major Lessons to Learn from Eph 1:1-14

- Ephesians is most likely a circular letter written to several churches in the Roman province of Asia, including possibly Colossae, Laodicea, and Hierapolis. However, because of the prominence of Ephesus and the church in Ephesus the epistle was most likely sent first to Ephesus then copied and sent the other churches. The message certainly does speak to the church in Ephesus, but is relevant to all churches in Asia.
- Paul praises God for what he has planned for the church; an eternal plan which he had in mind before the foundation of the earth.
- Out of his infinite love God chose (predestined) those who would be in Christ to be his children. This predestination is not Calvinistic predestination which is based on hereditary sin and total depravity (Calvinistic and Roman Catholic doctrines but not biblical doctrines).

In contrast to Calvinistic predestination the predestination spoken of by Paul is based on God's eternal love for mankind, his foreknowledge, and man's personal decision, faith, and obedience to the gospel.

- In Christ Christians have redemption and the forgiveness of sins according to the richness of God's grace.
- God's plan, spoken of as a mystery, is revealed in the gospel of Christ's death and resurrection and God's loving grace for all men. The plan reveals that God would unite both Jew and Gentile in Christ by grace through faith.
- God's purpose in all of this was that Christians would so live that they would bring glory to God in Christ and the church.
- The purpose of the Ephesian letter is to explain that Christians should live in a manner that brings glory to God through Jesus Christ.
- In Christ Christians have the fullness of their inheritance through the indwelling Holy Spirit. They do not need any special Gnostic intuitive knowledge in order to gain this. They already have all the knowledge and spiritual power *in Christ*.

Discussion Questions

- What is the basic difference between Calvinistic Predestination and Biblical Predestination?
- Discuss ways in which Christians can bring glory to God today?
- What does the term *Heilsgeschichte* mean? Give a modern day expression for this in terms of salvation or redemption.
- What was a basic philosophy of Gnosticism? Work off the meaning of gnosis.
- Are there any kind of "spiritual powers" active today? Name some that you may encounter in your life. What is the answer to these powers?

- How may this particular lesson from Ephesians apply today and how may it strengthen us today?

Lesson 6

Ephesians 1:15-23

The Laudation Continued
Paul's Prayer for the Ephesians and Christians in Asia

"15For this reason, because I have heard of your faith in the Lord Jesus and your love toward all the saints, 16 I do not cease to give thanks for you, remembering you in my prayers, 17 that the God of our Lord Jesus Christ, the Father of glory, may give you a spirit of wisdom and of revelation in the knowledge of him, 18 having the eyes of your hearts enlightened, that you may know what is the hope to which he has called you, what are the riches of his glorious inheritance in the saints, 19 and what is the immeasurable greatness of his power in us who believe, according to the working of his great might 20 which he accomplished in Christ when he raised him from the dead and made him sit at his right hand in the heavenly places, 21 far above all rule and authority and power and dominion, and above every name that is named, not only in this age but also in that which is to come; 22 and he has put all things under his feet and has made him the head over all things for the church, 23 which is his body, the fulness of him who fills all in all."

This *Laudatio* includes a prayer of concern for the recipients of the letter. This prayer is that God would give them a spirit of wisdom and a revelation of the knowledge of Christ so that they *would so live that they bring glory to God.* We will learn at Eph 3:14ff that Paul prays that the Christians would also receive the Holy Spirit working in their lives in order to help them and to empower them to bring glory to God.

Eph 1:15-23. The Greek of this section is in one long sentence with no period at the end of 1:17 as in the NIV.[11] The

---

[11] Andrew Lincoln observes, "The original Greek text of 1:15–23 forms one sentence. Again, for the sake of English style and intelligibility, the translation

RSV is correct in preserving the long sentence albeit with the understanding that this makes for difficult reading. In this long sentence, almost a paragraph, Paul introduces a theme that is vital to understanding both Ephesians and Colossians. We have already noticed that Paul's theological theme in Ephesians is that Christians should so live that they bring glory to God in Christ. However, in order to be able to live lives that bring glory to God in Christ two things are necessary.

First, contrary to Gnostic claims, Christians do not need a new form of esoteric knowledge; all they need is the correct knowledge of Christ. The right kind of knowledge focuses on what God has already done *in Christ*. He has already defeated the spiritual powers in the heavenly places through the death and resurrection of Jesus Christ. He has already provided Christians with the truth of their redemption, Jesus Christ. Cf. John 14:6 "*I am the way, and the truth, and the life; no one comes to the Father, but by me.*" The real truth about Jesus is that in Jesus all the divine power of divinity has already come to redeem them. Col 1:19, "*For in him all the fulness of God was pleased to dwell, [20] and through him to reconcile to himself all things, whether on earth or in heaven, making peace by the blood of his cross.*"

Second, Christians facing any powerful enemy while living in Christ will also need the power of the indwelling Holy Spirit. Note Paul's magnificent prayer at Eph 3:14-21:

> "*For this reason I bow my knees before the Father, [15] from whom every family in heaven and on earth is named, [16] that according to the riches of his glory he may grant you to be strengthened with might through his Spirit in the inner man, [17] and that Christ may dwell in your hearts through faith; that you, being rooted and grounded in love, [18] may have power to comprehend with*

---

has been broken down into a number of sentences and here the words "I pray" have been added in order to begin a new sentence." Lincoln, Ephesians, p. 47. Indicating the complexity of the punctuation of the text our Greek texts are divided as to whether or not a period appears following 1:19.

*all the saints what is the breadth and length and height
and depth, [19] and to know the love of Christ which
surpasses knowledge, that you may be filled with all the
fulness of God. [20] Now to him who by the power at work
within us is able to do far more abundantly than all that
we ask or think, [21] to him be glory in the church and in
Christ Jesus to all generations, for ever and ever. Amen."*

Thus, in this long extended sentence Paul addresses both the right kind of knowledge Christians need and the gift of the indwelling Holy Spirit which helps in understanding the knowledge of Christ and living to bring glory to God in Christ and the church.

Eph 1:15, Paul begins this pericope with the expression *"For this reason ..."* For what reason? For the reason that they have been destined by God to bring glory to him in Christ! He is tying the following verses back to 1:14 in which he had mentioned the indwelling Holy Spirit who is the guarantee of the Christian's inheritance. Paul mentions that he does not cease praying for the Ephesian Christians so that they will have a spirit of wisdom and knowledge in order to live so as to bring glory to God in Christ. To be able to do so they must have the right or correct knowledge.

Eph 1:17. Note the express words of Paul's prayer for the Christians, "that the God of our Lord Jesus Christ, the Father of glory, *may give you a spirit of wisdom and of revelation in the knowledge of him, having the eyes of your hearts enlightened* ..." Paul was well aware of the danger of the Gnostic appeal for special esoteric knowledge. He wanted the Christian's eyes of their heart (inner being) to be opened by the power of God and the knowledge of Jesus and not by some secret knowledge.

Paul is very aware of the Gnostic threat which claims to impart a special knowledge for the enlightened. He has already stated that in Christ God has provided the Christians with every spiritual blessing (Eph 1:3) they need. Now he adds that they should draw on the spiritual wisdom they have in the knowledge of Christ.

The word *knowledge*, ἐπίγνωσις, *epígnōsis*, implies *full knowledge[12]*. It was a term common in Gnostic philosophical thinking and had become a *technical term* in the mystery religious circles. For those of a Gnostic mindset it stood for some form of *special intuitive full knowledge of the ultimate god*. Gnostics held that in order to be one with the ultimate god one needed to have the intuitive secret full knowledge they had that would enable them to escape the powers of the universe. Paul argues that such full knowledge comes only from what God has revealed in Christ.

Eph 1:18-20. Paul prays for the Christians in Asia that *the eyes of their hearts might be enlightened*, not merely of their mind, but something that goes deeper than the mind. He prays that *"having the eyes of your hearts enlightened ... you may know what is the hope to which he has called you, what are the riches of his glorious inheritance in the saints, [19]and what is the immeasurable greatness of his power in us who believe, according to the working of his great might [20]which he accomplished in Christ when he raised him from the dead and made him sit at his right hand in the heavenly places ..."*

At **Eph 1:18.** Paul continued his long sentence building on the thought of the proper kind of knowledge the Christians in Asia needed. This right kind of knowledge lies simply in knowing *what God has done in Christ*.

Paul wanted the Ephesians to know what their true hope was. It was not some special mystical intuitive knowledge. It was simply Christ living in them and they in Christ! In a great text, parallel to the Ephesian concerns, at Colossians 1:24 ff Paul speaks of this hope "which is Christ in you" and not in some form of esoteric personal intuitive private knowledge:

---

[12] *Epígnōsis* is more intensive than *gnōsis* which simply means knowledge. *Epígnōsis* can express a more thorough participation in the acquiring of knowledge on the part of the learner. In the NT, it often refers to knowledge which very powerfully influences the form of religious life. Spiros Zodhiates, *The Complete Word study Dictionary: New Testament*.

"24 Now I rejoice in my sufferings for your sake, and in my flesh I complete what is lacking in Christ's afflictions for the sake of his body, that is, the church. 25 of which I became a minister according to the divine office which was given to me for you, to make the word of God fully known, 26 the mystery hidden for ages and generations but now made manifest to his saints. 27 To them God chose to make known how great among the Gentiles are the riches of the glory of this mystery, which is Christ in you, the hope of glory. 28 Him we proclaim, warning every man and teaching every man in all wisdom, that we may present every man mature in Christ. 29 For this I toil, striving with all the energy which he mightily inspires within me."

This reminds us today that we are not saved by our own knowledge and understanding of Scripture but by knowing that our salvation lies expressly in what God has done for us in Christ. Knowledge of Scripture, or the right knowledge of sound doctrine is important but it does not save us. It instructs us regarding what God has done in Christ but it is what God has done in Christ that saves us, not our knowledge. Knowledge is important, but it is the right kind of knowledge that counts! All knowledge including the knowledge of sound doctrine only informs us of what it is that really does save us, that is, God's gracious redeeming work in Christ. To think that our sound doctrine or knowledge of Scripture saves us is only a modern form of Gnosticism which focuses on the power of knowledge to save, but this was and is the Gnostics error. The right kind of knowledge or doctrine focuses on Jesus Christ who is the means and power of the Christian's salvation.

The right kind of knowledge is knowing that the power of our salvation lies in the power of Jesus' death, burial, and resurrection and of God's gracious redeeming work in Jesus.

Knowing Jesus does not simply mean knowing something about Jesus, but it involves entering into an appropriate relationship with Jesus through faith or trusting in Jesus and what God has done in Him.

Paul speaks of *the glorious inheritance in the saints* that God has worked for Christians. There is nothing that the Gnostic false teachers (or any false teachers) can offer Christians that is not already available for them in Christ.

Note how Peter in a different context makes the same point at 1 Pet 1:3:

> *"Blessed be the God and Father of our Lord Jesus Christ! By his great mercy we have been born anew to a living hope through the resurrection of Jesus Christ from the dead, ⁴ and to an inheritance which is imperishable, undefiled, and unfading, kept in heaven for you, ⁵ who by God's power are guarded through faith for a salvation ready to be revealed in the last time."*

Again at 2 Peter 1:3 Peter adds:

> *"His divine power has granted to us all things that pertain to life and godliness, through the knowledge of him who called us to his own glory and excellence, ⁴ by which he has granted to us his precious and very great promises, that through these you may escape from the corruption that is in the world because of passion, and become partakers of the divine nature."*

In the full knowledge of what God has done in Christ Christians have all the knowledge they need for life and godliness.

Eph 1:19. Paul wanted the Christians to know *the immeasurable power available to them* through what God had done for them in Christ, notable in the resurrection of Jesus. Again, we stress that Christians are not saved by knowledge but by the power of God seen in the cross of Christ and his resurrection.

Eph 1:20. All that Christians need for true knowledge is what God has already accomplished for them in Christ. Christians do not need any additional knowledge beyond Christ and what God has done for them in Christ in order to be saved and to bring glory to God. God has done all this by the working of his great might (Eph 1:20) "*when he raised him from the dead and made him sit at his right hand in the heavenly places …*"

This thought introduces a major point in Paul's message to the Ephesians, that is, Christ rules even in *the heavenly places*. *The heavenly places* may refer to views of the spiritual powers in the heavenly places with whom Paul was concerned. It is not special intuitive knowledge of these powers that saves the Christians, but the knowledge of what God has already done for them in Jesus Christ who already is ruling in the heavenly places. It is not the Gnostic demiurges of demigods who rule in the heavenly places; Christ does!

Christ has dominance over all spiritual powers whatever or wherever they may be! At his death and resurrection Jesus conquered Satan and all of Satan's spiritual powers. Cf. Matt 28:18, "*And Jesus came and said to them, "All authority in heaven and on earth has been given to me…"*

Eph 1:20 and the following verses clearly state that God has placed Jesus in control of all the heavenly places which in the Gnostic mind would include the realms over which the supposed demiurges or spiritual powers had control.

Jesus has absolute control of all the heavenly places. Such power does not reside in any supposed spiritual powers! God has placed Jesus at his right hand (a place of honor) in the heavenly places to rule over them.

As stated at Matt 28:18 Jesus has all rule and authority power and dominion for all ages over all creation, including any supposed spiritual powers such as the Gnostic demiurges. Paul drives this point home powerfully at Col 1:11-14 which was also written addressing similar concerns as in to the Ephesian epistle:

> "*May you be strengthened with all power, according to his glorious might, for all endurance and patience with joy, [12] giving thanks to the Father, who has qualified us to share in the inheritance of the saints in light. [13] He has delivered us from the dominion of darkness and*

transferred us to the kingdom of his beloved Son, [14] *in whom we have redemption, the forgiveness of sins."*

Paul enlarges on this at **Eph 1:22,** by stating that God has *"put all things under his feet and has made him the head over all things for the church,* [23] *which is his body, the fulness of him who fills all in all."*

That means he is sovereign ruler over everything including all spiritual powers in the heavenly places and on earth!

Notice a fine point here at vs 22! God has done this *for* the church, which is the body of Jesus. The concept of the church as the body of Christ is obviously prominent in Pauline theology and description of the church. Note especially Col 1:18, *"He is the head of the body, the church; he is the beginning, the first-born from the dead, that in everything he might be pre-eminent."* But the point Paul is stressing in the Ephesian text here is that God has made Jesus supreme over everything and has done this *for* the church, not simply *in* the church! *For the church, in behalf of the church, for the blessing and strengthening of the church,* God has set Jesus above all powers and rulers, either earthly or heavenly!

There is no power, demigod, or being that is above Jesus, including all spiritual powers, Satan, and agents of Satan. All are subject to him. They may be rebelling against him today, but all are under his authority and power and are subject to him. In the end all powers will bow their knee before Jesus and acknowledge him as Lord! Phil 2:11, *"Therefore God has highly exalted him and bestowed on him the name which is above every name,* [10] *that at the name of Jesus every knee should bow, in heaven and on earth and under the earth,* [11] *and every tongue confess that Jesus Christ is Lord, to the glory of God the Father."*

We know that Jesus defeated Satan on the cross and in his resurrection. John explains that Christians can defeat Satan today in their lives by their faithfulness to Jesus. Note this victorious statement of John's at Rev 12:10, 11:

And I heard a loud voice in heaven, saying, "Now the salvation and the power and the kingdom of our God and *the authority of his Christ **have come**, for the accuser of our brethren has been thrown down, who accuses them day and night before our God. [11]And **they have conquered him** by the blood of the Lamb and by the word of their testimony, for they loved not their lives even unto death." Cf. also Rom 8:35-39, "Who shall separate us from the love of Christ? Shall tribulation, or distress, or persecution, or famine, or nakedness, or peril, or sword? [36]As it is written, "For thy sake we are being killed all the day long; we are regarded as sheep to be slaughtered." [37]**No, in all these things we are more than conquerors through him who loved us.** [38]For I am sure that neither death, nor life, nor angels, nor principalities, nor things present, nor things to come, nor powers, [39]nor height, nor depth, nor anything else in all creation, will be able to separate us from the love of God in Christ Jesus our Lord."*

At **Eph 1:23** Paul concludes his long sentence by explaining that the church is the body of Christ and that *Jesus is the fulness of God.* He observes that *"the church which is his body is the fulness of him who fills all in all."*

First Paul stresses that *the church is the body of Christ.* Paul likes the analogy of the church/body. Note 1 Cor 12:12-27, in which Paul explains that those in the church are all individually members of one body and have all been baptized into the one body by the Holy Spirit. Note also Eph 4:4 where he adds that there is only one body (church), cf. Col 1:22. The point is that Christians have all been reconciled to God in the body of Christ, the church, which is the fulness of God's eternal purpose.

Second, the church/body is the *fulness* of God. *Fulness* is an important and loaded theological term! *Fulness* (Greek *plérōma*) was a favorite term among Gnostics and other philosophies in ancient times. It referred to *the fulness of deity.* Christians in Christ have reached *their full divine potential* in Christ. There is nothing more for the Ephesians and Christians to attain other than to be like Christ and God. Christians have already in Christ been transformed into the likeness of Christ and God and in Christ they continue every day through the power of the Holy Spirit to grow more like Christ. Christians have been united to Christ through baptism, and being born again in a new creation; Rom 6:1-11; John 3:3-5; Tit 3:5; 2 Cor 5:17. Now in Christ they grow to be more like him, reflecting his glory and the glory of God.

Third, the Gnostics and other religions have nothing they can offer that the Christians do not already have *fully in Christ*. Paul also develops this anti-Gnostic argument in his epistle to the Colossians in which he argues for the preeminence and all sufficiency of Christ. Note Col 1:15-20, In Christ *the fulness of God was pleased to dwell*:

> *[15] He is the image of the invisible God, the first-born of all creation; [16] for in him all things were created, in heaven and on earth, visible and invisible, whether thrones or dominions or principalities or authorities—all things were created through him and for him. [17] He is before all things, and in him all things hold together. [18] He is the head of the body, the church; he is the beginning, the first-born from the dead, that in everything he might be pre-eminent. [19] For in him all the fulness of God was pleased to dwell, [20] and through him to reconcile to himself all things, whether on earth or in heaven, making peace by the blood of his cross.*

When people are in Christ they share in the fulness of God in Christ. The Gnostics can offer nothing new or more than this!

Some Scholarly Observations Regarding this Pericope

All scholars observe that this text is very difficult to interpret in that it has some extremely difficult translation and syntactical issues! This study is not the place to unload these issues but the student is referred to the commentaries listed in the bibliography for further information. I will include three observations by three excellent scholars, Andrew Lincoln, Clinton Arnold and F. F. Bruce.

Andrew Lincoln in a comprehensive exegesis of Eph 1:22, 23 comments:

> "The final three clauses of the first chapter are some of the most difficult of the whole epistle for the commentator. Not only do they contain major problems of syntax and translation, but they also introduce key terms (head, church, body, and fullness), to which an immense amount of secondary literature has been devoted. The limits of this commentary forbid any full-scale review of and interaction with the literature, but an attempt will be made to sketch the broad outlines of such scholarly discussion ... Our decisions in regard to the three major areas of contention surrounding the last clause of the first chapter mean, then, that the writer's overall thought is that the church is Christ's fullness and that Christ is the one who is completely filling the cosmos. Here, as in 1:22b, ecclesiological and cosmic perspectives are juxtaposed in a way that underlines the Church's special status, for although Christ is in the process of filling the cosmos, at present it is only the Church which can actually be called his fullness. The Church appears, then, to be the focus for and medium of Christ's presence and rule in the cosmos."[13]

Arnold Clinton along similar lines observes regarding the several thoughts that Paul has introduced in this text:

> "In conclusion, the final clause of this section of the letter asserts that the church is filled with power and grace from its exalted Lord, who, in turn, extends his reign throughout heaven and earth through the church. The church accomplishes this through dependence on the one who fills her and by proclaiming the gospel and manifesting the kingdom of God to all in an extensive way."[14]

---

[13] Lincoln, *Ephesians*, p. 77.
[14] Arnold, Clinton E., *Ephesians, Zondervan Exegetical Commentary on the New Testament*, Eph 1:23, Zondervan. Kindle Edition, 2011.

Finally F. F. Bruce observes:

"But a more probable interpretation of the passive voice would be to take it as denoting the fact that in Christ the fullness of deity is perpetually resident. The grammatical problem will probably never reach a universally agreed solution, and we may content ourselves for the present with the rendering of the English versions. The Church, the body of Christ, is the complement of him who fills the entire universe."[15]

Major Lessons to Learn from Eph 1:15-23

- Paul begins the long, one sentence paragraph with *"For this reason ..."* which ties the paragraph and its message back to the reason for the epistle, that is, that Christians should so live that they bring glory to God in Christ. For this reason Paul prays that the Christians would have a spirit of wisdom and revelation in the knowledge of God and Jesus (not Gnostic special intuitive knowledge but knowledge of Christ) so they will know the real truth of what God has done for them in Christ.
- God has put Jesus over all authority and rule, including Satan and any other spiritual powers that Gnostics or others can conceive.
- Christians have everything they need in Christ who is the head over all things for the church.
- Christians reach the fulness of their potential in Christ who is himself the fulness of divine power and being.

Discussion Questions

- What advantage do Christians have over those outside of Christ as a result of the inheritance they have from God?
- Where does the Holy Spirit fit into the Christians life?

---

[15] Bruce, F.F. *The Epistle to the Ephesians: A Verse by Verse Exposition by One of the Great Bible Scholars of Our Age,* Kindle Edition, 2012. Italics IAF.

- Where can you reach your full potential in life? In financial prosperity, community and political power, position in employment? Discuss this thought more fully.
- In the past week how has the Holy Spirit helped you live your life for the glory of God? Be specific and practical.

Lesson 7

The Doctrinal Body of Ephesians

Eph 2:1-10

Saved by God's Grace through Faith in God's working in Jesus

[1] And you he made alive, when you were dead through the trespasses and sins [2] in which you once walked, following the course of this world, following the prince of the power of the air, the spirit that is now at work in the sons of disobedience. [3] Among these we all once lived in the passions of our flesh, following the desires of body and mind, and so we were by nature children of wrath, like the rest of mankind. [4] But God, who is rich in mercy, out of the great love with which he loved us, [5] even when we were dead through our trespasses, made us alive together with Christ (by grace you have been saved), [6] and raised us up with him, and made us sit with him in the heavenly places in Christ Jesus, [7] that in the coming ages he might show the immeasurable riches of his grace in kindness toward us in Christ Jesus. [8] For by grace you have been saved through faith; and this is not your own doing, it is the gift of God— [9] not because of works, lest any man should boast. [10] For we are his workmanship, created in Christ Jesus for good works, which God prepared beforehand, that we should walk in them.

Eph 2:1-7. Translating Eph 2:1-7 challenges the translators since there is no main verb in the sentence and one has to be supplied!

Notice Andrew Lincoln's comment on this in the *Word Biblical Commentary* on Ephesians:

> "The Greek text here does not have a finite verb but rather a participial clause, ὑμᾶς ὄντας νεκρούς…, lit. "you being dead…." In fact there is an anacoluthon in the Greek syntax, for this clause is the object of a verb

whose subject is introduced in v 4 but which itself does not appear until after the opening clause has been repeated in the first person plural in v 5, ὄντας ἡμᾶς νεκρούς, lit. "we being dead," and can then be seen to be συνεζωοποίησεν, "made alive with." In translating v 1, one can either supply the main verb from v 5—"And you he made alive, when you were dead"—and repeat this when one comes to v 5 (RSV) or simply translate the participle as a finite verb (NIV)."[16]

Lincoln's explanation is almost as difficult to read and understand as the Greek text itself! But it does draw attention to the difficulty in translating this sentence. He mentions an anacoluthon which complicates the flow of thought in the sentence.[17]

Where one inserts the main verb or supposed verb has shaped our different translations: NRSV – "You were dead through the trespasses and sins [2] in which you once lived…" RSV – "And you he made alive, when you were dead through the trespasses and sins…" NIV –"As for you, you were dead in your transgressions and sins…" KJV – "And you hath he quickened, who were dead in trespasses and sins…" NKJV – "And you He made alive, who were dead in trespasses and sins…"

However, in principle, in spite of the grammatical and syntactical issues the different translations read much the same! *Those who were dead in sins God has made alive in Christ*!
   Eph 2:1-3:
   [1]And you he made alive, when you were dead through the trespasses and sins [2]in which you once walked, following the course of this world, following the prince of

---

[16] Andrew Lincoln, *Ephesians*, Word Biblical Commentary, 1994, p. 84
[17] An anacoluthon is a clause or sentence in which the wording ignores the normal grammatical flow of words. It can result in syntactical or grammatical inconsistency or incoherence within a sentence as in a shift in an unfinished sentence from one construction to another. It might seem that the writer has dropped some words out or included something for emphasis. Syntax refers to how a sentence is constructed.

the power of the air, the spirit that is now at work in the sons of disobedience. [3]Among these we all once lived in the passions of our flesh, following the desires of body and mind, and so we were by nature children of wrath, like the rest of mankind."

Paul begins with the Greek word *kai, and,* which syntactically connects this section back to the *berakah blessing* of 1:3ff, and the theme of God's redemptive work in Christ. *"And"* since you are in Christ where you enjoy every spiritual blessing provided by God in his plan of salvation *"you he made alive, when you were dead through the trespasses and sins...."* We praise God (bless God) for planning our salvation, for calling us to be his children in Christ, *and (kai)* for bringing us to life when we were dead in sin! We who were dead in our sins now praise God for making us alive. (*Blessed or praised be the God...* Eph 1:3).

At one time these Christians (most likely Paul has in mind the Gentile Christians for he picks up this thought again at Eph 2:11, *"at one time you Gentiles..."*) were dead in their sins, *having no hope in the world* (Eph 2:12), and *alienated from the commonwealth of Israel. Dead* or death here refers to *total destruction or ruin.* It does not simply refer to spiritual death or physical death. It means they were in a state of *total ruin!* Without God and Christ in their lives they were totally "lost" without any hope. Now they are saved, children of God, alive in Christ (Eph 2:11ff.).

Eph 2:4-7:

"[4]But God, who is rich in mercy, out of the great love with which he loved us, [5] even when we were dead through our trespasses, made us alive together with Christ (by grace you have been saved), [6] and raised us up with him, and made us sit with him in the heavenly places in Christ Jesus [7] that in the coming ages he might show the immeasurable riches of his grace in kindness toward us in Christ Jesus."

But now *in Christ* by God's great love and mercy they have been *made alive together with Christ*. Several commentators believe the reference here to being dead and now made alive with Christ refers to Christian baptism (cf. Rom 6:1-11; Col 2:12, 13)[18]. At one time the Gentiles had been under the power of the prince of the power of the air – a reference to Gnostic understanding of evil. Now in Christ they were freed from such powers.

Note particularly Paul's reference to baptism at Col 2:12, 13:

> "... *and you were buried with him in baptism, in which you were also raised with him through faith in the working of God, who raised him from the dead.* [13] *And you, who were dead in trespasses and the uncircumcision of your flesh, God made alive together with him, having forgiven us all our trespasses,* [14] *having canceled the bond which stood against us with its legal demands; this he set aside, nailing it to the cross.* [15] *He disarmed the principalities and powers and made a public example of them, triumphing over them in him."*

The result of Jesus' death on the cross and consequent resurrection is that he reigns supremely over Satan, having conquered Satan especially in his resurrection. He reigns over the heavenly places, and over all creation. Through Christians being united with his death and resurrection they have been made alive and reign with him! God has done all this so that in the coming ages (that is, after his coming, παρουσία, *parousia*[19]) he might show us the immeasurable riches of his grace and kindness.

---

[18] Lincoln, *Ephesians*, p. 101 f; Arnold, *Exegetical Commentary on Ephesians*, Eph 2:5; Peter O'Brian, *The Letter to the Ephesians*, Eph 2:5, 6. The commentators may not mention Christian baptism but most tied this text at Eph 2:4-6 to passages tied to baptism such as Rom 6:1-4 and Col 2:12, 13.

[19] Παρουσία, *parousia*; to be present, presence, a being present, a coming to a place, coming or arrival. Spiros Zodhiates, *The Complete Word Study Dictionary, New Testament*.

Eph 2:8, 9. In this text we have one of the best known and most often quoted verses of the Bible:

> *"8For by grace you have been saved through faith; and this is not your own doing, it is the gift of God — 9not because of works, lest any man should boast. 10For we are his workmanship, created in Christ Jesus for good works, which God prepared beforehand, that we should walk in them."*

Driving home the point that our salvation lies in the working of God and not our knowledge, Paul stresses that we are saved by God's grace through faith in the workmanship of God. Paul also develops this theme of salvation or justification by grace through faith in his letter to the Romans, especially in Rom3:21-26:

> *"21 But now the righteousness of God has been manifested apart from law, although the law and the prophets bear witness to it, 22 the righteousness of God through faith in Jesus Christ for all who believe. For there is no distinction; 23 since all have sinned and fall short of the glory of God, 24 they are justified by his grace as a gift, through the redemption which is in Christ Jesus, 25 whom God put forward as an expiation by his blood, to be received by faith. This was to show God's righteousness, because in his divine forbearance he had passed over former sins; 26 it was to prove at the present time that he himself is righteous and that he justifies him who has faith in Jesus."*

Salvation is the gift of God. It lies in his working and our faith in his working and our obedience to him. We do not receive it or earn it by our works, by keeping the Law of Moses, or even works done in righteousness. Neither do we receive it by receiving a special intuitive knowledge. We receive our salvation simply by God's grace and through our faith in Jesus and God's working in our salvation.

Note that this text does not say that faith is the gift of God! It is salvation that is the gift of God. Some, especially of the "faith only" Calvinistic view of salvation argue that since man is totally depraved he cannot on his own even believe. Faith it is argued is in this view is therefore the gracious gift of God to the unbeliever. However, that is not what this text is saying! This text states quite clearly that we are saved by God's grace through our faith in Jesus! It is salvation that is the gift of God in his text, not faith.

It is a fundamental biblical doctrine that our salvation is a gift of God which we receive through our faith in the working of God. Paul states this quite clearly at Col 2:12-14:

> "... and you were buried with him in baptism, in which you were also raised with him **through faith in the working of God**, who raised him from the dead. [13]And you, who were dead in trespasses and the uncircumcision of your flesh, God made alive together with him, having forgiven us all our trespasses."

Paul clearly teaches that in baptism we are saved and raised with Christ *through faith (trusting) in the working of God*, and not by our own works.

Jew and Gentile are united in one Body by the Cross of Jesus Eph 2:11-21

This is a long pericope! And it is profoundly important to Paul's message to the Ephesians and to Paul's theology of salvation, redemption, and reconciliation:

> "[11]Therefore remember that at one time you Gentiles in the flesh, called the uncircumcision by what is called the circumcision, which is made in the flesh by hands— [12]remember that you were at that time separated from Christ, alienated from the commonwealth of Israel, and strangers to the covenants of promise, having no hope and without God in the world. [13]But now in Christ Jesus you who once were far off have been brought near in the blood of Christ. [14]For he is our peace, who has made us both one, and has broken down the dividing wall of hostility, [15]by abolishing in his flesh the law of

commandments and ordinances, that he might create in himself one new man in place of the two, so making peace, [16] and might reconcile us both to God in one body through the cross, thereby bringing the hostility to an end. [17] And he came and preached peace to you who were far off and peace to those who were near; [18] for through him we both have access in one Spirit to the Father. [19] So then you are no longer strangers and sojourners, but you are fellow citizens with the saints and members of the household of God, [20] built upon the foundation of the apostles and prophets, Christ Jesus himself being the cornerstone, [21] in whom the whole structure is joined together and grows into a holy temple in the Lord; [22] in whom you also are built into it for a dwelling place of God in the Spirit."

The major point is that God has reconciled all people, Jew and Gentile, to himself in and through Jesus Christ. Those in Christ are not divided, but have been united in one body by the cross. It is because of the death of Jesus Christ on the cross and his resurrection that both Jew and Gentile are reconciled to God in one body since we are all baptized by one Spirit into his one body, the church, 1 Cor 12:12, 13 ff. Our salvation comes not by keeping the Law of Moses or through some esoteric knowledge. It comes only in and through Jesus Christ. Note particularly how Paul developed this in Gal 3:23-29. I have set certain words in bold letters for emphasis:

*"Now before faith came, we were confined under the law, kept under restraint until faith should be revealed. [24] So that the law was our custodian until Christ came, that we might be justified by faith. [25] But now that faith has come, we are no longer under a custodian; [26] **for in Christ Jesus you are all sons of God, through faith. [27] For as many of you as were baptized into Christ have put on Christ. [28] There is neither Jew nor Greek, there is neither slave nor free, there is neither male nor female; for you are all one in Christ Jesus. [29] And if you are***

Christ's, then you are Abraham's offspring, heirs according to promise."

Paul now takes up this emphasis at **Eph 2:11.** The word *therefore* takes us back to Eph 2:1-10 and stands in parallel to that text's message. You Gentiles were dead in your sins and God has made you alive in Christ. *Now remember* that at one time you were separated from Christ, etc.

The Jews who held to a *circumcision made by hands* (circumcision was a sign of a covenant relationship with God) called the Gentiles the *uncircumcised* in that they were in the Jewish view Gentiles and not part of the covenant relationship God made with Abraham and which was carried forward in the Law of Moses. The Jews however forgot or rejected the point that the Gentiles were included by God in the covenant he had made with Abraham at Gen 12:1 ff and Gen 17:1ff.

Eph 2:12. In their previous sinful condition Gentiles were separated from Christ, alienated from the commonwealth of Israel, strangers to the covenant promise, having no hope without God in the world. *They were lost!*

Eph 2:13. The interesting Greek conjunctive expression νυνὶ δὲ, *nuni de, but now,* stresses the fact that *now*[20] in the Christian or eschatological age things have changed. *Now* in Christ, those who had been far removed from God by their sin are *now* brought near to God in the blood of Christ. *In Christ* all people are saved, both Jew and Gentile, both the circumcised and the uncircumcised, *all are saved together in one body by God's grace through faith in Jesus Christ.*

Eph 2:14-16. Christ made the difference by abolishing the Law[21] which had in some measure separated Jew from Gentile,

---

[20] The little expression νυνὶ δὲ, *nuní de* derived from νῦν, *nún* is an *adverbial* phrase when *nún* is strengthened by the demonstrative *i* (iota). It forms an interesting technical theological term. Scholars call this an eschatological *nún, now,* implying that the redemption of the Gentiles in Christ refers to the present eschatological age introduced by Christ, or as we might call it, the final Christian age of God's plan of salvation.

[21] For discussion of the annulment of the old Law cf. Heb 8:9-10:10.

and made peace with God for both Jew and Gentile by the cross. In fact, God had never intended the Law of Moses to be a boundary marker between the Jew and Gentile, but the Jews had made it such. God had always intended his covenant relationship with Israel to be based on faith, not Law. This is the story of Romans and Galatians.

However, in the mind of the Jew the Law of Moses represented a covenant relationship between only God and the Jews. However, the Law of Moses had been instituted to clarify for God's covenant people the nature and consequences of sin. Cf. Gal 3:19, 26-29 where Paul had argued that the covenant between God and Abraham was not based on the Law of Moses but on faith, and was intended for both Jew and Gentile.

In practice the law had become a dividing wall between Jew and Gentile, but now since the Law had been abolished that wall had been removed by the cross. In Christ God had united both Jew and Gentile as one new "man". There was now no longer two "men" (Jew and Gentile) but one new "man" (Christians in Christ).

Where animosity and hostility had existed, now peace should reign. Both Jew and Gentile are reconciled to God *in one body by the cross*.

Eph 2:17-19. Jesus had come and preached peace for and between all people. Through Jesus we all, both Jew and Gentile, have access in one Spirit to the Father.

Two things: *First*, note the Trinitarian function in this text. Christ, the Father, and the Holy Spirit.

Second, note the emphasis on the Spirit and the unity of both Jew and Gentile (Cf. 1 Cor 12: 13; we are all baptized by one Spirit into one body, both Jews and Greeks). Jews and Gentiles in Christ are no longer enemies or strangers, but are one family, fellow citizens with all the other saints in God's house.

Eph 2:20, 21. Paul mixes his metaphors of family and house, using now the analogy of a house or building. The church or family of God is built on the foundation of the apostles and prophets (this is a genitive of apposition in which the apostles and prophets are the foundation) with Jesus being the cornerstone by which the building is aligned.

The point here is that both the apostles (by their teaching the gospel of Jesus and the cross) and Jesus form the foundation of the church, but Jesus is the aligning principle, the cornerstone of the foundation and church.

In Jesus (*in whom*) all are joined together like stones in a building into one holy temple (*in the Lord*) in which both Jews and Gentiles become a dwelling place of God in the Spirit. *Note the heavy emphasis on unity of all believers in this text.*

Major Lessons to Learn from Eph 2:1-2:21

- Paul continues the thought he had developed in Eph 2:1-10, namely that we are all children of God and saved by grace through faith in Jesus Christ. We have been created in Christ for good works in which we should walk (live).
- *Therefore*, we should *remember* from where we have come, where we were strangers and alienated from God, lost, and without hope in the world.
- Christ's death has changed things and now we all are brought together in one body by the cross (the death and resurrection of Jesus). It is not by our works or Law keeping that we have been brought together in one body, but solely by God's grace and our faith in his working.
- We are all fellow citizens in Christ, joined together and forming one holy temple in the Lord.
- The main point is to remember our lost past condition and what God has done for us. We have been united by His grace and His Holy Spirit and form one body in Christ, the church.

Discussion Questions

- Remember and recount your experience of conversion to Christ.

- How has your life changed as a result of that conversion experience?
- Can you think of times and conditions when you or we as Christians have not been one in Christ?
- How can this text help us when we have problems in the church that tend to divide us?

Lesson 8

Ephesians 3:1-21
The Doctrinal Body of Ephesians Continued

The Function and Purpose of the Church

Eph 3:1 -13.

"¹For this reason I, Paul, a prisoner for Christ Jesus on behalf of you Gentiles— ² assuming that you have heard of the stewardship of God's grace that was given to me for you, ³ how the mystery was made known to me by revelation, as I have written briefly. ⁴ When you read this you can perceive my insight into the mystery of Christ, ⁵ which was not made known to the sons of men in other generations as it has now been revealed to his holy apostles and prophets by the Spirit; ⁶ that is, how the Gentiles are fellow heirs, members of the same body, and partakers of the promise in Christ Jesus through the gospel. ⁷ Of this gospel I was made a minister according to the gift of God's grace which was given me by the working of his power. ⁸ To me, though I am the very least of all the saints, this grace was given, to preach to the Gentiles the unsearchable riches of Christ, ⁹ and to make all men see what is the plan of the mystery hidden for ages in God who created all things; ¹⁰ that through the church the manifold wisdom of God might now be made known to the principalities and powers in the heavenly places. ¹¹ This was according to the eternal purpose which he has realized in Christ Jesus our Lord, ¹² in whom we have boldness and confidence of access through our faith in him. ¹³ So I ask you not to lose heart over what I am suffering for you, which is your glory."

Note again how Paul begins this chapter or section. *"For this reason ..."* He is returning to the theological theme of Ephesians, but before he gets too deeply into this he introduces a new thought. The anacoluthon at the end of vs. 1 and just before vs.2, is interesting, *"For this reason I, Paul, a prisoner for Christ Jesus on behalf of you Gentiles— [2] assuming that you have heard..."* The anacoluthon which begins with *"assuming that you have heard..."* is a break in thought where the writer wishes to introduce a parenthetical thought into the discussion. Paul will return to the original thought at Eph 3:14. In our bible text the anacoluthon is indicated by a long "dash" --. Determining the end of the anacoluthon is sometimes difficult but is arrived at by examining the context of the discussion.

The *anacoluthon* is best understood as ending at the end of Eph 3:13. Eph 3:2-13 is therefore a *parenthetical* thought that Paul introduces to amplify something that he thinks needs explanation.

Paul will again return to the expression *"for this reason"* at Eph 3:14 indicating that he is picking up the thought introduced at Eph 3:1. He will explain at Eph 3:14 that *the reason he prays* (*bows the knee before the Father*) is that the Christians may be strengthened with might in their inner person (man). But why does he pray this prayer? He prays for the Christians so that they, called by God as part of his eternal purpose and who are destined to so live for the purpose of bringing glory to God through Jesus Christ, *may have power to live that they bring glory to God.* To bring glory to God is the destiny, purpose, and function of Christians, so *for this reason* Paul prays that they may be strengthened with might in order to be able to fulfill their divinely ordained and appointed purpose!

Now we need to examine Paul's parenthetical thought. Parenthetical thoughts are important which is why the writer introduces the parenthesis!

Eph 3:2-13. This long pericope is the parenthetical thought in which Paul digresses from his main thought to introduce a new but important emphasis:

> *"-- assuming that you have heard of the stewardship of God's grace that was given to me for you, [3] how the mystery was made known to me by revelation, as I have written briefly. [4] When you read this you can perceive my*

insight into the mystery of Christ, [5] which was not made known to the sons of men in other generations as it has now been revealed to his holy apostles and prophets by the Spirit; [6] that is, how the Gentiles are fellow heirs, members of the same body, and partakers of the promise in Christ Jesus through the gospel.

[7] Of this gospel I was made a minister according to the gift of God's grace which was given me by the working of his power. [8] To me, though I am the very least of all the saints, this grace was given, to preach to the Gentiles the unsearchable riches of Christ, [9] and to make all men see what is the plan of the mystery hidden for ages in God who created all things; [10] that through the church the manifold wisdom of God might now be made known to the principalities and powers in the heavenly places.

[11] This was according to the eternal purpose which he has realized in Christ Jesus our Lord, [12] in whom we have boldness and confidence of access through our faith in him. [13] So I ask you not to lose heart over what I am suffering for you, which is your glory."

Eph 3:2, 3. The new thought is to emphasize that by God's grace he, Paul, had been appointed as a special apostle to the Gentiles. Paul does this to stress the thought introduced at Eph 2:11ff that the Gentiles are important and that God's purpose was that both Jews and Gentiles would be reconciled in one body by the cross. How God would do this had been a mystery in the past to both Jew and Gentile; but this mystery now had been revealed to Paul and the apostles by God.

Paul purposefully emphasized that he had received this mystery and commission to preach to the Gentiles by a revelation from God. This underscores the importance of his ministry and preaching to the Gentiles. It also highlights again that the mystery Paul referred to was how God was going to unite both Jew and Gentile in one body. What had been a mystery was now revealed in Paul's preaching of the death and resurrection of Jesus.

Eph 3:4-8. The mystery was that the Jews and Gentiles were to be *fellow heirs* of God's promises and covenant to Abraham which had been fulfilled in Jesus on the cross. The church as the body of Christ was the "place" where Jew and Gentile would be united. This Paul describes was a revelation of *the unsearchable riches of God in Christ*. Paul explains that he was not worthy of this magnificent and significant message but that *out of God's grace* he had been granted the privilege of preaching this great and precious mystery. Notice the repeated emphasis of what God has done *in Christ*.

Eph 3:9-13. It was God's intention that all men should see and understand this mystery. Being united in one body by the cross would demonstrate to the world God's mysterious plan, wisdom, and power. Naturally, this would be contingent on the Jew and Gentile being committed to living in unity in the church, cf. Eph 4:1ff.

Demonstrating God's plan by living together in harmony in the church would be the church's ministry of revealing God's plan to all creation, including the "principalities and powers in the heavenly places". Paul had been granted the honor of preaching this mystery; now it was the church's responsibility to demonstrate this mystery by the members of the body, Jew and Gentile, living in peaceful harmony.

Note this emphasis: It is *in and by the life function* and *behavior* of the church that the world will be able to see God's great plan and *the riches of God in Christ*.

Paul explains in this text that it is not simply through the church's *preaching ministry* that the church demonstrates and proclaims this mystery. It is primarily through *the manner in which the church maintains the unity of the Spirit in the bond of peace* (Eph 4:1-6) that the world will see the mystery and plan of God demonstrated before them. It is when the world can see Jews and Gentiles (multi-ethnic groups) behaving as God's children in unity in the one church that God's plan is revealed and the church brings glory to God.

Paul's Prayer for the Saints

Eph 3:14-21

This pericope is one of the great texts of Ephesians. With a prayer for the saints Paul ends his anacoluthon and parenthesis and returns to his major theme and concern that the Christians understand their primary purpose of bringing glory to God through Jesus Christ and the church:

> *"For this reason I bow my knees before the Father,*
> [15] *from whom every family in heaven and on earth is named,* [16] *that according to the riches of his glory he may grant you to be strengthened with might through his Spirit in the inner man,* [17] *and that Christ may dwell in your hearts through faith; that you, being rooted and grounded in love,* [18] *may have power to comprehend with all the saints what is the breadth and length and height and depth,* [19] *and to know the love of Christ which surpasses knowledge, that you may be filled with all the fulness of God.* [20] *Now to him who by the power at work within us is able to do far more abundantly than all that we ask or think,* [21] *to him be glory in the church and in Christ Jesus to all generations, for ever and ever. Amen."*

The leading thought of this prayer is that Christians may be powerfully strengthened with might in their inner being so that they may be able to fulfill their destiny [eternal purpose] of bringing glory to God.

This prayer is in the form of a benedictory[22] prayer to the doctrinal section of Ephesians. After expressing this prayer Paul moves on to the paranetic section of the epistle in Eph 4:1 ff. He highlights the importance of the theology of his epistle with the

---

[22] A benediction from the Latin *bene* (good, well, quite right, in good style, better, best) and *dictum* (saying) which refers in religious contexts to a short prayer for divine help, pronounces s blessing, and calls for guidance. It usually is found at the end of worship service or at the end of a major theological statement or teaching.

highly liturgical intercessory prayer for God's divine intervention through his Holy Spirit.

In this prayer Paul underscores the important point that all people are equally members of the universal family of God (Eph 3: 15). This sets the prayer in a context that accentuates his point that both Jew and Gentile are equal in the sight of God and both have equal rights to God's blessings.

The "cosmic" fatherhood of God was held not only by Jews but also by several leading Greek philosophers such as Plato and Philo. It would resonate well with the Ephesian and Asian Greek Gentiles.

Lincoln discusses at length the cosmic setting of this prayer which draws on the universal fatherhood of God:

> "To extol God the Father as father of all family groupings in heaven and on earth is to set his fatherhood in the context of creation and of the cosmos. The idea of the cosmic father of all who is creator of all can be found elsewhere in, for example, Plato, *Timaeus* 28C, 37C, 41A; Philo, *Spec.* 2.165; 3.189; or *Corpus Hermeticum* 5.9; 11.6–8; 12.15b; 14.4. Explicit statements of God's universal fatherhood are not found elsewhere in the Pauline corpus, but a similar formulation occurs again later in this letter in 4:6, "one God and Father of all," and the thought has been prepared for by the reference in 3:9 to "God who created all things."[23]

Note the major thoughts of Paul's prayer; he calls on the riches of God's glory in Christ; he prays that God would strengthen the Ephesians and all other Christians in their inner being through the indwelling Holy Spirit; he prays that Christ may dwell in their hearts through faith; he prays that they may be grounded in love since without Christian love no unity can exist, especially between Jew and Gentile; he prays that together with all the saints they may have power to comprehend and know [experience] what is the extent of the love of Christ which passes

---

[23] Lincoln, *Ephesians*, p. 203.

all human understanding; he prays that they may be filled with all the *fullness* of God. *Fullness (plĕrōma*[24]*)* was a concept the Gnostics played with and stood for the fullness of spiritual blessing and knowledge of the divine.

The final statement of Eph 3:20, 21 gets to the heart of Paul's concern for the Ephesian Christians and emphasizes that *through the indwelling Holy Spirit God empowers Christians to "do far more abundantly than they ask or think."* The piling up of *far more abundantly* emphasizes the powerful promise of the indwelling Holy Spirit!

What this means *first* is that God is the Father of all mankind, Jew and Gentile, even of the angels, and *second* that as we make an effort to be one body in Christ through faith in Jesus Christ God thorough His Holy Spirit will empower us to be the kind of people we want to be and he wants us to be. We make the effort by faith and God strengthens this effort through the power of the Holy Spirit who dwells in us. Thus by the help of the Holy Spirit we are empowered to bring glory to God in one family through the church and in Christ.

The context of this whole pericope (Eph 3:1-21) highlights the point that unless Jew and Gentile can live together in unity the world and the spiritual powers in the heavenly places will not learn of and see God's wisdom and the riches of God's glory in Christ.

It is only when the church lives in unity and harmony that Satan and the spiritual powers, as well as our neighbors, can see God's glory working in and through the church.

Paul recognized that for the Jew and Gentile Christians to live together in harmony in the church it would call for a supreme effort in order to shed centuries of animosity. In order to do this the church needed to know that *first* this was God's foreordained and predestined will and plan for the church; *second* the Ephesian Christians needed to make every effort to

---

[24]*Plĕrōma,* πλήρωμα, *plĕrōma* was a popular term in Greek philosophic and religious tradition which meant fulness, but typically in the Gnostic tradition, the fulness of deity.

achieve this; and *third*, God would strengthen them in their inner person thorough his indwelling Holy Spirit in order to reach this goal.

Paul develops this major thought of the unity of the body of Christ, which is the church, in the next chapter.

Major Lessons to Learn from Eph 3:1-21

- Notice Paul's use of the expression "For this reason ..." He is tying this section back to the theology of Ephesians that Christians should so live that they bring glory to God in Christ.
- However, before he does so he embarks on an anacoluthon in which he explains his apostolic ministry to the Gentiles and the mystery of God. Paul's ministry was to preach and reveal that mystery.
- The mystery was how God was going to reconcile both Jew and Gentile to himself in one body, one church. For centuries the Jew and Gentile had lived in animosity toward one another. The point Paul makes is that outside of Christ the Gentiles were estranged from God (cf. 2:11ff) and could only be reconciled together with the Jews in the one body of Christ.
- The mystery was that God would reconcile them in one body, the church, through Jesus Christ and his cross.
- When in the church, both Jew and Gentile live in peace, then the church by its example manifests the wisdom of God's plan to the world.
- Paul recognized that Christians would need additional help to overcome centuries of animosity so he explains that God has given his Holy Spirit to dwell in Christians to empower them to maintain unity and to do far more than they could ever expect.

Discussion Questions

- Discuss the thought introduced by Paul with his expression "For this reason ..." For what reason?

- What is the main thrust of the anacoluthon of Eph 3:2-13?
- How does Paul explain that the church would manifest the wisdom of God to the world?
- How does this apply to the church today?
- What instances or occasions in church life today could negate the church's ministry in this regard?
- Explain how the Holy Spirit works in the life of the Christian. Comment on Phil 2:12, 13.

Lesson 9

Ephesians 4:1-4:16
The Practical Body of Ephesians

Introduction

One important lesson we learn from studying Paul is that he never gave theological or doctrinal instruction without explaining its practical implications. The practical instruction that applies a doctrinal or theological thought to life we call a *paranesis*. *Paranesis* refers to moral, ethical and practical application of doctrinal or theological statements. For Paul *paranesis* is always anchored in doctrinal or theological concepts.

Eph 4:1-6:20 constitutes the *paranetic* material of the epistle which builds on the theology of the Ephesian epistle. If the theological center of the Ephesian epistle is that *Christians are destined to so live that they bring glory to God in Christ*, then the paranetic material should explain *how* this should be done.

The first point of the *paranetic* material in Ephesians demonstrates a central concern of God, Paul, and the epistle. It notably highlights Paul's major concern for the churches in Asia, and everywhere, *the unity of the church.* That this is the first point in the paranetic material accentuates its importance. *How* Christians should bring glory to God by living in *unity* in the church should be a prime concern of all Christians and the church. *Christians (Jews and Gentiles) must make every effort to maintain the unity of the Spirit and live in the one body of Christ, the church, in a peaceful relationship.*

The Unity of the Church (4:1-16)

¹I therefore, a prisoner for the Lord, beg you to lead a life worthy of the calling to which you have been called, ²with all lowliness and meekness, with patience, forbearing one another in love, ³eager to maintain the unity of the Spirit in the bond of peace. ⁴There is one body and one Spirit, just as you were called to the one

hope that belongs to your call, ⁵ one Lord, one faith, one baptism, ⁶ one God and Father of us all, who is above all and through all and in all. ⁷ But grace was given to each of us according to the measure of Christ's gift.
⁸ Therefore it is said, "When he ascended on high he led a host of captives, and he gave gifts to men." ⁹ (In saying, "He ascended," what does it mean but that he had also descended into the lower parts of the earth? ¹⁰ He who descended is he who also ascended far above all the heavens, that he might fill all things.) ¹¹ And his gifts were that some should be apostles, some prophets, some evangelists, some pastors and teachers, ¹² to equip the saints for the work of ministry, for building up the body of Christ, ¹³ until we all attain to the unity of the faith and of the knowledge of the Son of God, to mature manhood, to the measure of the stature of the fulness of Christ; ¹⁴ so that we may no longer be children, tossed to and fro and carried about with every wind of doctrine, by the cunning of men, by their craftiness in deceitful wiles. ¹⁵ Rather, speaking the truth in love, we are to grow up in every way into him who is the head, into Christ. ¹⁶ from whom the whole body, joined and knit together by every joint with which it is supplied, when each part is working properly, makes bodily growth and upbuilds itself in love."

Paul begins this first and possibly the major paranetic material by explaining *how* Christians, Jews and Gentiles, can begin to go about bringing glory to God through Christ and in the church. In this important pericope he speaks of *maintaining the unity of the Spirit in the bond of peace*. Lincoln introduces this pericope with an appropriate title, *The Church's Calling to Maintenance of the Unity It Already Possesses*.²⁵ The point Lincoln makes is most appropriate to the sense of the pericope. He calls on them to maintain the unity *they already possess*!

---

²⁵ Lincoln, *Ephesians*, p. 221.

This unity is the unity of the one body of Christ into which they have all been baptized by the one Holy Spirit.

This continuing emphasis on the work of the Holy Spirit is important to both Paul's theology, the theology of the kingdom, and the theology of this epistle. At 1 Cor 12:12, 13 Paul had taught the Corinthians that all Christians are baptized by the one Holy Spirit into one body, the church:

> "[12] For just as the body is one and has many members, and all the members of the body, though many, are one body, so it is with Christ. [13] For by one Spirit we were all baptized into one body—Jews or Greeks, slaves or free—and all were made to drink of one Spirit…"

Now in the first paragraph of the paranetic material, **Eph 4:1-2**, Paul *begs, exhorts, strongly urges,* the Christians to *lead a life worthy* of their *calling.* The Greek, παρακαλέω, *parakaléō,* means *to call on,* to *summon, to invite, to urge, to implore, to beg, which implies a strong calling or urging.*[26]

Paul had already established that their calling which had been predestined by God, was that they should live for the praise of God's glory. Paul is reminding them precisely of that calling.

The point Paul will make here is that maintaining the unity of the Spirit in the bond of peace (Eph 4:3) is *how* Christians live a life *worthy of their calling and bring glory to God. They live a life worthy of their calling when they maintain the unity of the body in peace and so bring glory to God in Christ.*

We are reminded that the theology of Ephesians is that Christians have been *called* by God in Christ (and destined) to *so live their lives that they bring glory to God* in Christ (Eph 1:3ff).

In this pivotal pericope Paul is emphasizing how important it is for Christians to live in unity without which they cannot bring glory to God in Christ. That they are to do this as the first paranetic emphasis in his epistle, underscores this as being of first in importance! Unfortunately the history of the church

---

[26] Spiros Zodhiates, *The Complete Word Study Dictionary: New Testament;* Lincoln, Ephesians, pp. 225 f has an great discussion of this paranetic material and the use of the expression *I beg.*

indicates that this has not been a major concern of some churches, especially in the history the modern Restoration Movement.

Paul accentuates this by stressing that Christians are to be *eager to maintain the unity of the Spirit "with all lowliness and meekness, with patience, forbearing one another in love"*.

Lowliness, ταπεινοφροσύνης, *tapeinophrosúnēs* means *a quality of voluntary submission and humility, unselfishness, or self-effacement*[27]. That means counting oneself less or lower than other people.

Meekness, πραΰτης, *praütēs* means *gentleness, courtesy, and humility*. The doubling up of these almost synonyms is interesting. In the Greek *lowliness* and *meekness* are joined in a grammatical construction by a coordinating conjunction, *kai* forming what is referred to as *hendiadys*[28] which unites the two concepts lowliness and meekness, as one. Paul is calling for a spirit of *voluntary meek unselfish humility and lowliness.*

In the Greco-Roman world such lowliness and servitude was not highly praised and was considered *contemptible servility* and not a characteristic to be admired. In contrast to this in the Judeo-Christian world, including such Jewish sectarian views as the Essenes of the Dead Sea communities such an attitude of humility and lowliness was highly praised.

To these two mindsets of humility Paul adds *patience*, μακροθυμία, *makrothumía; to be long–suffering, forbearing, self–restraint before proceeding to action.* Long-suffering is the quality of a person who is able to avenge himself yet refrains

---

[27] A more complete definition would be, low-minded, base, lowly, humble, lowliness of mind, the esteeming of oneself as small, inasmuch as we are small. Spiros Zodhiates, *The Complete Word Study Dictionary: New Testament.*

[28] Two nouns, noun forms, verbs or verb forms in the same case of tense joined by *kai*, *and*, speak of one thing through two things, with the second noun functioning as an adjective to the first noun!

from doing so[29]. Christians are to be longsuffering and patient with one another.

Then to this Paul piles more on, adding *forbearing one another in love. Forbearing* derives from ἀνέχομαι, *anéchomai, putting up with, enduring, and accepting.* The driving influence in this forbearance is love, ἀγάπη, *agápē, affectionate regard, goodwill, benevolence, desiring the best for the other person*[30]. All of these qualities are *rational cognitive decisions; being willing to consider and put the other person first; getting along together.* We will learn that they are also relational in the sense that all Christians are children of God in Christ, both Jew and Gentile. *Christians are one family.*

At **Eph 4:3** Paul introduces a primary ingredient to the discussion which is that in a spirit of lowliness and humility Christians *must be eager to maintain the unity of the Spirit in the bond of peace.*

Christians as children called by God to be his sons in Christ must be *eager* to maintain this unity. *Eager* derives from σπουδάζω *spoudázō* meaning *in a hurry, doing one's best, making every effort, earnestness, diligence.* Christians *must make every effort* to maintain the unity of the Spirit. Andrew Lincoln observes, "Spare no effort; make it a priority for your corporate life to maintain the unity of the Spirit." Such an exhortation also makes plain that the unity of the Spirit is a reality that is to be demonstrated visibly.[31]

However, in keeping with the previous qualities, they are to do this in *the bond of peace. Bond* derives from σύνδεσμος, *súndesmos* which means *a link or joint or bond.* There is something that *bonds* or *links* Christians to this unity. *The bonding agent is peace. Peace* derives from εἰρήνη, *eirḗnē,* and carries the *sense of spiritual or inner tranquility.* Εἰρήνη, *eirḗnē*

---

[29] Spiros Zodhiates, *The Complete Word Study Dictionary: New Testament.*

[30] Spiros Zodhiates, *The Complete Word Study Dictionary: New Testament;* Kittel, *Theological Dictionary of the New Testament,* Vol. 1, pp. 22 ff.

[31] Lincoln, *Ephesians,* Word Biblical Commentary, 1990, p. 237; Peter O'Brian, *The Letter to the Ephesians,* Ephesians 4:1-3.

stands in opposition to hostility or conflict. There is to be no hostility or conflict between all Christians as God's *called children. Hostility destroys unity!*

Eph 4:3. Paul does not state that Christians *create or bring about* this unity. They *maintain* the unity *that the Holy Spirit has created* or brought about.

Paul speaks of *the unity of the Spirit.* The prepositional phrase ἑνότητα τοῦ πνεύματος, *enoteta tou pneumatos,* is a genitive construction which in this case is a subjective genitive which implies that *the unity comes from the Spirit. The unity is created by the working of the Spirit. This unity is not our creation!* Christians are to protect, preserve, and maintain *the unity that already exists* as a result of the working of God's Holy Spirit! In this case the unity is a unity that *belongs to* the Holy Spirit or which is *derived from* the Holy Spirit.   Andrew Lincoln remarks:

> "The unity of the Spirit involves not the human spirit but the Holy Spirit, as v 4 makes clear, and is a reference not to the congeniality of some social grouping but to the unity which God's Spirit gives and which is the ground of the Church's existence. The term ἡνότης, "unity," occurs in the NT only here and in v 13 but it becomes a basic Christian concept later in Ignatius (e.g., Eph. 4.2; 5.1; 14.1...). So whereas Col 3:14, 15 refer generally to love and peace, Ephesians distinctively and more specifically speaks of unity. Although this unity is already given and is not therefore the readers' own achievement, it must be preserved and protected."[32]

We need to comment further on the kind of *unity* implied. What kind of unity does Paul have in mind here? In Eph 4:3 and 13 Paul will discuss two kinds of unity; the one which we already have in Christ and the other into which we must grow in Christ! I will refer to these as an *ontological* unity and a *cognitive* unity.

---

[32] Lincoln, *Ephesians*, p. 237, Peter O'Brian *The Letter to the Ephesians*, Ephesians 4:1-3,

The word unity derives from ἑνότης, *henótēs, which in turn derives from heís* which simply means *one.* Thus *henótēs* or *unity* meaning *oneness*, or simply as we translate it, *unity.*

At the root of *henótēs* lies two Greek words, the first *hēs, mia, hen* which are the three gender noun forms of *one.* The other root form is *ontos, eimi* which basically means *to be* or *to exist.* Thus *henótēs* primarily means *to be one, to exist as one,* hence *oneness* or *unity.*

Now the unity referred to in Eph 4:3 is not a *cognitive unity* of *knowledge or faith* into which one grows over time, but an *ontological unity of being* into which we have been born. Specifically *we are one in being, one in identity, one in body.*

Later at Eph 4:13 Paul will speak of a *unity of faith and knowledge. This is a cognitive unity.* We will discuss this unity in the next lesson, but basically it means a unity of knowledge and faith which both imply growth in the future life of the Christian.

At **Eph 4:3** Paul speaks of *maintaining* or *preserving the unity which the Spirit has created.* This unity has been brought about by the work of the Holy Spirit. All Christians have (Jew and Gentile) been baptized by the *one Spirit into one body* (1 Cor 12:13). This takes place at our conversion and new birth when we are born of water and spirit (John 3:3-5, Tit 3:4-7). Luke points out at Acts 2:38 that when we believe, repent, and are baptized we receive the Holy Spirit as a gift. This is all part of the working of God through the Holy Spirit in our new birth. By the work of the Holy Spirit we are born again into the one family of God, and consequently baptized into the one body of Christ.

In keeping with Paul's thinking in Ephesians, note 2 Thess 2:13, 14:

> *"But we are bound to give thanks to God always for you, brethren beloved by the Lord, because God chose you from the beginning to be saved, through sanctification by the Spirit and belief in the truth.* [14]*To this he called you through our gospel, so that you may obtain the glory of our Lord Jesus Christ..."*

Thus all Christians (in the context of Ephesians, notably Jews and Gentiles) are *called* by God and *destined* (expected) *to live in unity* and *maintain the unity* brought about by the power of God and the work of the Holy Spirit at their new birth into the born again family of God. By living in the unity of the Spirit we bring glory to God for his magnificent plan to unite all in one body by the cross and work of the Holy Spirit.

Eph 4:4-6 explains the theological foundation for this unity:

> *"There is one body and one Spirit, just as you were called to the one hope that belongs to your call, ⁵one Lord, one faith, one baptism, ⁶one God and Father of us all, who is above all and through all and in all."*

Backing into this verse from its end we observe that if there is only one God, one Lord Jesus Christ, one Holy Spirit, one baptism, and one faith in Jesus, one hope in Jesus, one body of Christ, *there can be only one body, one church.*

There is one Father for both Jew and Gentile, therefore there can be only one family of God. There is only one Lord Jesus, therefore there can be only one body of Christ, one church belonging to Christ. There is not a church for the Jew and a church for the Gentile. *There is only one church*! A church divided by ethnic diversity (or any division) cannot be the one church that belongs to Jesus. *It cannot therefore bring glory to God.*

Note Andrew Lincoln's discussion of this interesting collection of *ones*:

> "The Church's unity, already expressed in terms of the unity of the Spirit, is now asserted through a series of seven acclamations of oneness. These fall into two groups of three, plus a concluding acclamation of the one God with its own fourfold repetition of the word "all." For discussion of the use of traditional material here, see Form/Structure/Setting. The sequence of thought can be said to move from the Church, as the writer's most immediate concern, on to the Church's Lord and then on to God himself. This sequence corresponds to a number

of the patterns of thought earlier in the letter. But the precise sequence is dictated more by compositional and rhetorical factors than by any deliberate preference for experiential rather than logical order in creedal formulation ... There is a Hellenistic Jewish background to formulations about oneness in general and formulations about the oneness of God (v 6) in particular. For example, 2 Apoc. Bar. 85.14 can state, "Therefore, there is one law by One, one world and one end for all who exist," while Philo, Spec. 1.67, talks of there being one sanctuary because there is only one God. The oneness of God was, of course, a topic in Jewish diaspora propaganda (cf., e.g., 2 Macc 7:37; Philo. Leg. Alleg. 2.1; Josephus, Ant. 5.1. 25 § 97; 8.13.6 § 343; Ag. Ap. 2.23 § 193; Sib. Or. 3.11; 3.629; cf. also E. Peterson, ΕΙΣ ΘΕΟΣ [Göttingen: Vandenhoeck & Ruprecht, 1926] esp. 141–48, 254–56). Particularly interesting as parallels are passages which derive the unity of the Jewish people from the oneness of God. Philo, Virt. 7.35, asserts that "the highest and greatest source of this unanimity is their creed of a single God, through which, as from a fountain, they feel a love for each other, uniting them in an indissoluble bond" (cf. also Spec. 1.52; 4.159, and 2 Apoc. Bar. 48.23, 24, which claims "we are all one people of the Name; we, who received one law from the One"). For the writer of Ephesians also there is a clear link between the unity of the Church and the various acclamations of oneness in vv 4–6. The behavior for which he has called, the maintenance of the unity of the Spirit, can now be seen to be the only consistent practical expression of the foundational unities he enumerates here. At the same time, by reminding his readers of these distinctive realities to which they are committed, he reinforces both the sense of cohesion he wants them to have as members of the Church and the sense of their distinctive identity vis-à-vis the surrounding society."[33]

Introducing a new dynamic into the discussion at **Eph 4:7-16** Paul now explains that God through Christ has given gifts to the church to enable the church members *to grow in their faith into a cognitive* unity and *maturing ministry* so that they can bring glory to God through their maturing faith in Jesus and developing lives dedicated to the ministry of God.

In **Eph 4:8-10** Paul uses an analogy of conquering kings who give gifts to their soldiers. He then follows it up with the fascinating discussion of Jesus who descended to earth and then ascended back to heaven. The background to this is possibly the Gnostic myth of a teacher who would come from the cosmic heaven above down to earth to bring special knowledge and truth. Jesus has done that very thing! As our conquering king he has given the church all of the spiritual gifts they may need. Remember Eph 1:3, he has blessed us in Christ with every spiritual blessing. There is no need to look for further kind of spiritual enlightenment and giftedness that Christians do not already have in Christ! As we will now learn a major aspect of that giftedness is that he has given the church apostles, prophets, evangelists, and teaching pastors to enrich the church's faith and help them grow in faith and ministry!

Eph 4:11 explains that the gifts Jesus gave to the church are the teaching ministry of the church who "*equip the saints for the work of ministry*". To be specific these gifts of teaching ministry were that some would be *apostles*, some *prophets* (inspired spokespersons for God), some *evangelists*, and some *pastors and teachers*. All of these ministry gifts function in a teaching ministry whose purpose is for the maturing of the faith and service of the members.

Apostles referenced here were those chosen by Christ and commissioned by him to be the first leaders and evangelists in the church. They were *sent out* by Jesus, cf. Acts 1:8, the word

---

[33] Andrew Lincoln, *Ephesians,* pp. 237f.

ἀποστέλλω, *apostéllō* means to be sent out with authority to represent the sender. The noun form of this verb is ἀπόστολος, *apóstolos* which refers to one sent out on a mission or commissioned to carry out some duty.[34] Certain men were specifically chosen by Jesus to be his chosen and empowered emissaries or apostles to begin the ministry of evangelism and maturing the church. We refer to these as the apostles of Christ.

Prophets, from the Greek προφήτης, *prophétēs*, were inspired speakers who could testify to the truth of a message. "… the prophet spoke not his own thoughts but what he received from God, retaining, however, his own consciousness and self-possession [35] The prophets of the Old Testament and New Testament were inspired by God's Holy Spirit to speak his message clearly and with authority. Cf. 2 Pet 1:19-21:

> *"And we have the prophetic word made more sure. You will do well to pay attention to this as to a lamp shining in a dark place, until the day dawns and the morning star rises in your hearts. [20] First of all you must understand this, that no prophecy of scripture is a matter of one's own interpretation. [21] because no prophecy ever came by the impulse of man, but men moved by the Holy Spirit spoke from God."*

Evangelists from εὐαγγελιστής, *euaggelistés (pronounced euangelistays)* were the proclaimers or teachers of the gospel, that is, the *good news* concerning Christ. In other words they would be preaching ministers or evangelists in the church today. The gospel as we will learn in Ephesians was the message they proclaimed that according to the predestined will of God Jesus

---

[34] "An apostle, *one sent, apostle, ambassador*. Sometimes used syn. with *presbeutés*, an ambassador, The messenger or ambassador … can never be greater than the one who sends him … The Lord chose the term *apóstoloi* to indicate the distinctive relation of the Twelve Apostles whom He chose to be His witnesses … Therefore, it designates the office as instituted by Christ to witness of Him before the world (John 17:18). It also designates the authority which those called to this office possess." Spiros Zodhiates, *The Complete Word Study Dictionary: New Testament.*

[35] Spiros Zodhiates, *The Complete Word Study Dictionary: New Testament.*

had died on a cross and been raised from the dead to enable those who were dead in sin to be made alive in Christ through faith in the working of God (Eph 2:1-10).

The expression *pastors and teachers*, ποιμένας καὶ διδασκάλους, *poimenas kai didaskalous*, is in an interesting construction which as I mentioned above we call *hendiadys* in which two nouns are connected by a coordinating conjunction, *kai*, and are tied together as one concept. The second word acts as an adjective defining the first word. Thus *pastors and teachers* means *teaching pastors*. The word *pastor* is from the Greek ποιμήν, *poimén* and is the Greek word for *shepherd*. In the New Testament *pastors are* not the preachers but the *shepherds* or *elders of the flock*. There are three words that describe the work of an elder. They are *elder* (πρεσβύτερος, *presbúteros*) *bishop* (ἐπίσκοπος, *epískopos*, sometimes translated as *overseer*) and *shepherd* (*poimén*). They are used interchangeably to describe the different function of this ministry. Cf. Acts 20:28; 1 Pet 5:1-3.

The point here is that these *pastors* are *teaching pastors* or *teaching elders*. One of the qualities of a bishop or elder is that he must be "*apt to teach*" (1 Tim 3:2) meaning not only capable but also willing to teach.

Each of these four ministries (apostles, prophets, evangelists, teaching pastors) given by Christ as a gift to the church are primarily a *teaching ministry*. Through their teaching and example apostles, prophets, evangelists, and elders "*equip the saints for the work of ministry*". They also serve in "*building up the body of Christ*" (the church). These four teaching ministries are for equipping the saints for the work or ministry or serving others in the body of Christ. They are "*to equip the saints for the work of ministry, for building up the body of Christ, [13] until we all attain to the unity of the faith and of the knowledge of the Son of God, to mature manhood, to the measure of the stature of the fulness of Christ*", Eph 4:12, 13.

The goal of this teaching and equipping ministry is that Christians "*attain to the unity of the faith and of the knowledge* of the Son of God". This unity is *not* referring to the *ontological* unity of Eph 4:1-6, but to a *cognitive* unity into which Christians must all *grow and mature* [Eph 4:13, 14]. It refers to a unity of faith and a unity of knowledge, both of which come as a result of teaching, growth and maturity.

Lincoln[36] draws attention to the difference in the unity being discussed in Eph 4:3 and the unity of Eph 4:13. The first unity, the ontological unity, is the working of the Holy Spirit. The second unity, the cognitive unity, is the work of the teaching ministries mentioned in Eph 4:11, that of the teaching of the apostles, prophets, evangelists, and teaching pastors. The unity discussed in Eph 4:13 is one of progression toward the mind of Christ including faith in the sense of sound doctrinal understanding of Christ in contrast to that which results from the false teachers encountered in Ephesus and Asia. One should remember that Ephesians was written regarding true faith in the pagan world of Artemis, the mystery religions, and Gnosticism. Gnosticism denied that the Christ had come in the flesh; that Jesus in the flesh was not the Christ or Redeemer of Light.

In the body of Christ Christians all share in the same *ontological* unity of the Spirit, we are all equally members of the body of Christ, the church. There is no difference between Jews and Gentiles (God shows no partiality in salvation between Jew and Gentile, Rom 2:10, 11; and Gal 3:28). However, we have not all reached the same *cognitive unity of faith and knowledge*. The teaching ministry of the church is for the purpose of our edification, growth, and maturing in faith. However, even in the cognitive realm Christians must strive to maintain the unity of the body of Christ.

Eph 4:15. "*Speaking the truth in love*" we are to grow up into maturity in Christ who is the head of the body, the church, teaching and speaking to one another in love.

Eph 4:16. From our relationship with our head, Jesus Christ, the whole body functions in *unison* (a *functional* unity) when

---

[36] Lincoln, *Ephesians*, p. 254 ff; Peter O'Brian, *The Letter to the Ephesians*, Ephesians 4:7-13.

every member (Jew and Gentile) is *"joined and knit together"*. Being joined together in Christ *we grow and build one another up in love*.

Major Lessons to Learn from Eph 4:1-16

- This chapter is where Paul begins the practical (*paranetic*) application of the doctrinal part of the letter.
- The doctrinal part of the letter stressed that Christians are called and destined to so live that they bring glory to God in the church.
- To enable them to do this effectively and thereby manifest to the world the mystery and glory of God he has given us his Holy Spirit to empower us to live for his glory in a practical manner, for this is our calling.
- First, we are called to so live that we maintain the unity of the Spirit in the bond of peace. This is an ontological unity of our being God's children.
- Paul explains that Christ has given gifts to the church of teachers who can equip the church for ministry and growth to where they have a cognitive unity of faith and knowledge of Jesus.
- The equipped and mature body of Christ results when every Christian (Jew and Gentile) is knit together and functions in unison.

Discussion Questions

- How does the unity of the Spirit come about? Cite some Scriptures that explain this.
- What attitudes are needed for Christians to be able to maintain this unity?
- What does Paul explain regarding the ministry of apostles, prophets, evangelists, and elders in this text?
- What might three major goals be as a result of this teaching ministry?

- In the context of this lesson how do Christians manifest the glory of God in Christ? Be practical. Stay in the context of Ephesians 4!

Lesson 10

Ephesians 4:17-5:20
The Practical Body of Ephesians Continued

The Moral Standards of the Church

Paul was well aware of the low moral standards of the Asian (especially the Ephesian) pagan Gentile culture. At **Eph 4:17-32** He explains that in order to bring glory to God through Christ and the church Christians must learn to live according to different standard of morals than their pagan neighbors.

"[17] Now this I affirm and testify in the Lord, that you must no longer live as the Gentiles do, in the futility of their minds; [18] they are darkened in their understanding, alienated from the life of God because of the ignorance that is in them, due to their hardness of heart; [19] they have become callous and have given themselves up to licentiousness, greedy to practice every kind of uncleanness. [20] You did not so learn Christ!— [21] assuming that you have heard about him and were taught in him, as the truth is in Jesus. [22] Put off your old nature which belongs to your former manner of life and is corrupt through deceitful lusts, [23] and be renewed in the spirit of your minds, [24] and put on the new nature, created after the likeness of God in true righteousness and holiness.

[25] Therefore, putting away falsehood, let every one speak the truth with his neighbor, for we are members one of another. [26] Be angry but do not sin; do not let the sun go down on your anger, [27] and give no opportunity to the devil. [28] Let the thief no longer steal, but rather let him labor, doing honest work with his hands, so that he may be able to give to those in need. [29] Let no evil talk come out of your mouths, but only such as is good for edifying, as fits the occasion, that it may impart grace to those who hear. [30] And do not grieve the Holy Spirit of God, in

whom you were sealed for the day of redemption. [31] Let all bitterness and wrath and anger and clamor and slander be put away from you, with all malice, [32] and be kind to one another, tenderhearted, forgiving one another, as God in Christ forgave you."

Eph 4:17, 18. Paul describes the pagan Gentile culture as being *darkened* and *alienated from God* (cf. 2:11 ff). Remember that the Platonic Gnostic philosophy taught that mankind lives in darkness and needs a special intuitive knowledge to escape from the evil world and evil powers of the heavenly places. The Gnostics were correct in concluding that the world is evil, but it was an evil world for a reason different from the Gnostic views and their solution to this evil was wrong!

Contrary to Gnostic and other philosophic solutions, Christ had already conquered the evil power in the world and Christians had already received all the special knowledge in Christ that they need to escape the evil world and its forces. They have been recreated (reborn) in the image of God and Christ. At Col 1:13 Paul clearly stated that God *"has (already[37]) delivered us from the dominion of darkness and transferred us to the kingdom of his beloved Son, [14] in whom we have redemption, the forgiveness of sins."* At Col 3:9, 10 he adds that Christians *"have put off the old nature with its practices [10]and have put on the new nature, which is being renewed in knowledge after the image of its creator."*

Eph 4:19-22. As former pagan Gentiles the Christians had been callous, licentious, and greedy and prone to practice all kinds of immorality. But this is not what they had learned in Christ! Paul follows this with another anacoluthon (parenthetical statement) *"assuming that you have heard about him and were taught in him, as the truth is in Jesus".* He encourages the

---

[37] The tense of the word *delivered*, ἐρρύσατο, being an aorist verb from ῥύομαι, *rhúomai*, "to draw or snatch from danger, rescue, deliver", implies a past action. Spiros Zodhiates, *The Complete Word Study Dictionary: New Testament.*

Christians to *put off their former manner of life* and follow Christ.

Eph 4:23, 24. Paul reminds the Christians that they have already been taught to live differently from their Gentile pagan neighbors. They have been *renewed in the spirit of their minds.* They have been *recreated* into new creatures (cf. Rom 6:1-11; Eph 4:23; Col3:10; 2 Cor 3:18). They have been created in *the likeness of God.*

Eph 4:25-29. Falsehood and anger should not be part of the Christian's makeup. Christians must *learn to speak truth to one another,* to *treat one another properly,* to *use their speech to edify* (build up) *one another,* and to *impart grace to one another. Anger* should not be permitted to linger in the Christian's life. Christians with the help of the Holy Spirit must learn to control emotions such as anger, cf. Ps 37:8f. Christians must be careful not to give occasions to the devil by careless lives. Falsehood, anger, and evil talk (most likely with a sexually immoral implication) should not be part of the Christian's speech. Christian speech and communication should *impart grace to the hearer* and not set a bad example of communicating and fostering immorality. Pau warns that God's Holy Spirit who dwells in us and empowers us to live a Christian life is grieved by immoral talk and behavior.

Eph 4:30-32. Christians should not by their unkind actions (notably in their Jewish and Gentile traditional attitudes toward one another) grieve the Holy Spirit who is present in their lives and who has brought them together into one body. They must be *"kind to one another, tenderhearted, forgiving one another, as God in Christ forgave"* them.

Eph 5:1-20. In this section Paul develops the moral characteristics necessary to bringing glory to God in Christ and the church. *Christians must be imitators of God* who loved them (both Jew and Gentile) and *forgave them equally* (Gal 3:25-29).

Eph 5:1-20 reads:

"*[1] Therefore be imitators of God, as beloved children. [2] And walk in love, as Christ loved us and gave himself up for us, a fragrant offering and sacrifice to God.*

[3] But fornication and all impurity or covetousness must not even be named among you, as is fitting among saints. [4] Let there be no filthiness, nor silly talk, nor levity, which are not fitting: but instead let there be thanksgiving. [5] Be sure of this, that no fornicator or impure man, or one who is covetous (that is, an idolater), has any inheritance in the kingdom of Christ and of God. [6] Let no one deceive you with empty words, for it is because of these things that the wrath of God comes upon the sons of disobedience. [7] Therefore do not associate with them, [8] for once you were darkness, but now you are light in the Lord; walk as children of light [9] (for the fruit of light is found in all that is good and right and true), [10] and try to learn what is pleasing to the Lord. [11] Take no part in the unfruitful works of darkness, but instead expose them. [12] For it is a shame even to speak of the things that they do in secret; [13] but when anything is exposed by the light it becomes visible, for anything that becomes visible is light. [14] Therefore it is said,

"Awake, O sleeper, and arise from the dead, and Christ shall give you light."

[15] Look carefully then how you walk, not as unwise men but as wise, [16] making the most of the time, because the days are evil. [17] Therefore do not be foolish, but understand what the will of the Lord is. [18] And do not get drunk with wine, for that is debauchery; but be filled with the Spirit, [19] addressing one another in psalms and hymns and spiritual songs, singing and making melody to the Lord with all your heart, [20] always and for everything giving thanks in the name of our Lord Jesus Christ to God the Father."

Eph 5:1, 2. Christians must *walk* περιπατέω, *peripatéō,*[38] (live) in love. Love, ἀγάπη, *agápē, affectionate regard, goodwill, benevolence, the desire for the very best for the other,*[39] accentuates the point that Christians should forgive one another just as Christ and God have forgiven them.

Note that the moral life of Christians is modelled on Jesus Christ's life example and God's holy nature. Peter at 1 Peter 1:15-17 had encouraged Christians in the Diaspora to be holy in their living, "[15] but as he who called you is holy, be holy yourselves in all your conduct; [16] since it is written, "You shall be holy, for I am holy." Christians should make every effort to live as God desires them to live and not as the world lives, especially the pagan world.

Eph 5:3-6. Pagan immorality must not be part of the Christian experience. Remember from our introduction the mention of the immoral sexual practices of the fertility cult of Artemis and the presence of a major brothel on the main street in Ephesus. Sexual immorality was a deep seated part of Ephesian life. Ephesus was a sea port and consequently a hub of immoral life. The *filthiness, levity,* and *silly talk* Paul mentions here all have to do with sexual impurity.

The Greek word translated *fornication* at the opening of this paragraph (Eph 5:3) is πορνεία *porneía,* which means *to commit fornication or any sexual sin, lewdness, or any other sexual impropriety.*[40] No fornicator or sexually impure person has any part in the kingdom of God. At Rom 1:18-32 Paul enlarges on a pagan life lived in rebellion against God and states that God's wrath will come on those who are disobedient and who practice

---

[38] Literally περιπατέω *peripatéō*; means to walk, to tread or walk about, generally to walk. However, figuratively it means to live or pass one's life. Spiros Zodhiates, *The Complete Word Study Dictionary: New Testament.*
[39] Spiros Zodhiates, *The Complete Word Study Dictionary: New Testament.* Cf. the other major Greek-English Lexicons in the bibliography. This love is not simply an emotional love but a cognitive decision in favor of the other.
[40] Spiros Zodhiates, *The Complete Word Study Dictionary: New Testament.*

immorality. Note also Paul's comments on sexual immorality and the kingdom at 1 Co 6:9-12:

> "Do you not know that the unrighteous will not inherit the kingdom of God? Do not be deceived: neither the immoral, nor idolaters, nor adulterers, nor sexual perverts, [10] nor thieves, nor the greedy, nor drunkards, nor revilers, nor robbers will inherit the kingdom of God. [11] And such were some of you. But you were washed, you were sanctified, you were justified in the name of the Lord Jesus Christ and in the Spirit of our God."

Eph 5:7. Christians must not *associate* (συμμέτοχος, *summetochos, be a participant, be caught up in a close accepting relationship*[41]) with pagans *who live immoral lives.* Cf. 1Cor 5:9-13:

> "I wrote to you in my letter not to associate with immoral men: [10] not at all meaning the immoral of this world, or the greedy and robbers, or idolaters, since then you would need to go out of the world. [11] But rather I wrote to you not to associate with any one who bears the name of brother if he is guilty of immorality or greed, or is an idolater, reviler, drunkard, or robber—not even to eat with such a one. [12] For what have I to do with judging outsiders? Is it not those inside the church whom you are to judge? [13] God judges those outside. "Drive out the wicked person from among you."

Eph 5:8, 9. Christians are children of light, not darkness. Remember that Gnostics considered the world to be in darkness and for light to come from the God of Pure Light through some form of intuitive knowledge. Christians as children of the God of pure light must live in the light of God.

Eph 5:10. Christians as children of their heavenly father must try to learn what is pleasing to the Lord, and to do what is pleasing to him.

---

[41] Spiros Zodhiates, *The Complete Word Study Dictionary: New Testament.*

Eph 5:11-14. Christians should not even *speak* of the things the Gentiles speak of. In their speech they should keep as far away as possible from the things of darkness, notably sexually permeated immoral speech. Regarding the danger of speech and the tongue as the agent of speech we are reminded of James' comment at James 3:1 ff that the tongue can if not carefully controlled be destructive.

Eph 5:15-17. Christians must be careful how they live, not as unwise people but as wise persons, fully aware of what is going on and the results of an immoral life. They must *make the most of their time*. This expression is interesting, ἐξαγοραζόμενοι τὸν καιρόν, *exagoradzomenoi ton kairon* literally means *buying up the time*. ἐξαγοραζόμενοι, *exagoradzomenoi* derives from *ek* and *agora* which mean *out of the marketplace*. The expression becomes a metaphor for *buying*. The word καιρός, *kairós* means *significant, urgent time*. Some translations render this expression as *making the most of the time*, others simply as *'buying up the time''*. It simply means that Christians should not be foolish and careless with their time and lives. They should make the most of their precious time for as Paul adds *"the days are evil."*

Eph 5:18, 19. Christians should not live in pagan debauchery. The expression *"drunk with wine"* refers to drunken debauchery especially associated with the mystery cults. In contrast to being filled with wine and *under the influence of wine*, Christians should be *filled with the Spirit* and under *the influence of the things of the Spirit* who dwells in them. The cultural context of Paul's admonition was the pagan mystery religions, especially the celebration to Bacchus, the god of wine, and the drunken debauchery of pagan celebrations. In contrast to pagan debauchery and drunken singing, Christians should sing songs of praise to God. They should join in the celebration of God, not pagan celebration.

They should sing *"psalms, hymns, and spiritual songs"* rather than drunken songs. This is considered to be a summary of the kind of songs sung by Christians. They should make *melody in their heart* singing praises to God and Jesus and not in a drunken stupor like the pagans.

It is debatable whether Paul is referring to singing in the worship services in this text or merely to the Christians general response to the Holy Spirit in contrast to the response to drunken debauchery. The view of some scholars is that the liturgical language used is that of the worship assembly, but not all agree on this!

This is not the place to debate or discuss the role of *acappella*[42] singing or singing accompanied by an instrument in the public worship assembly. Suffice it to say here that there is sufficient evidence in the use of the words *psallō*, ψάλλω, *psállō* and ᾄδω, *ádō* in the New Testament and early Christian practice to identify this singing and the meaning of the word *psallō* and its related word *adō* to support the practice of singing *acappella* in the worship assembly of the church[43].

Eph 5:20. Paul encourages the Christians with the expression *"always and for everything giving thanks in the name of our Lord Jesus Christ to God the Father."* It is debated whether this verse should be attached to this paragraph or begin the next paragraph as will be discussed in the next lesson. Many scholars see this verse as a transitional verse between Eph 5:1-19 and Paul's instruction of living a moral life and Eph 5:21 ff in which he gives instruction of the ideal family life. However, wherever it is placed it emphasizes that the joy of Christian life is expressed in giving thanks to God and Jesus Christ for all they have done in saving Christians and calling them to be God's children in Christ.

---

[42] *Acappella* is derived from the Latin/Italian and literally means "in the manner of the church" or "in the manner of the chapel". It refers to singing unaccompanied by any musical instrument which was the practice of the early churches and still is among Eastern Orthodox churches.
[43] Cf. Rubel Shelly, *Sing Praise! A Case for A cappella Music as Worship Today*; Everett Ferguson, *A Cappella Music in the Public Worship of the Church*; Everett Ferguson, Jack P. Lewis, Earl West, *The Instrumental Music Issue*.

Major Lessons to Learn from Eph 4:17-5:20

- This lesson continues the paranetic material that results from the doctrinal material emphasized in Eph 1:3-3:21. It explains how Christians bring glory to God through their practical and moral living.
- It calls Christians to a higher moral standard than that practiced by their pagan or unbelieving neighbors.
- No worldly uncleanness should be permitted to linger in Christian lives.
- Christians should be careful not to grieve the Holy Spirit who dwells in them and is given to empower them to live better lives for Christ and the glory of God.
- Anger, falsehood, filthy talk should not be permitted to reside in the Christian.
- Christians must make the most of their time and not use their time carelessly (buying up the time).
- The Christian life and joy should be the overflowing of a Spirit filled life and not the response of wine in drunken debauchery as was common in Ephesus and Asian life. Under the influence of a Spirit filled life Christians should sing psalms and hymns of praise to God. Remember Paul and Silas in the Philippian jail (Acts 16:25ff).

Discussion Questions

- What moral issues do you see as a major problem to Christian witness in today's culture?
- How can Christians address such issues?
- List some of the thoughts that impacted you in this study.
- Name some practical helps tools in overcoming anger in one's life?
- Eph 5:1 encourages Christians to be imitators of God. What is the context of Paul's encouragement? In this context how can we be imitators of God and what impact will this have on others?

Lesson 11

Ephesians 5:21-6:20
The Practical Body of Ephesians Continued

The Christian House Rules

Eph 5:21-6:9

[21] Be subject to one another out of reverence for Christ. [22] Wives, be subject to your husbands, as to the Lord. [23] For the husband is the head of the wife as Christ is the head of the church, his body, and is himself its Savior. [24] As the church is subject to Christ, so let wives also be subject in everything to their husbands. [25] Husbands, love your wives, as Christ loved the church and gave himself up for her, [26] that he might sanctify her, having cleansed her by the washing of water with the word, [27] that he might present the church to himself in splendor, without spot or wrinkle or any such thing, that she might be holy and without blemish. [28] Even so husbands should love their wives as their own bodies. He who loves his wife loves himself. [29] For no man ever hates his own flesh, but nourishes and cherishes it, as Christ does the church, [30] because we are members of his body. [31] "For this reason a man shall leave his father and mother and be joined to his wife, and the two shall become one flesh." [32] This mystery is a profound one, and I am saying that it refers to Christ and the church; [33] however, let each one of you love his wife as himself, and let the wife see that she respects her husband. [6:1] Children, obey your parents in the Lord, for this is right. [2] "Honor your father and mother" (this is the first commandment with a promise). [3] "that it may be well with you and that you may live long on the earth." [4] Fathers, do not provoke your children to anger, but bring them up in the discipline and instruction of the Lord. [5] Slaves, be obedient to those who are your

*earthly masters, with fear and trembling, in singleness of
heart, as to Christ; [6] not in the way of eye-service, as
men-pleasers, but as servants of Christ. doing the will of
God from the heart, [7] rendering service with a good will
as to the Lord and not to men. [8] knowing that whatever
good any one does, he will receive the same again from
the Lord, whether he is a slave or free. [9] Masters. do the
same to them, and forbear threatening. knowing that he
who is both their Master and yours is in heaven, and that
there is no partiality with him. "*

The Greek syntax of **Eph 5:21** is closely connected to **5:20**
indicating that the expression *be subject to one another* is a result
of *a life of thanksgiving to the Father* and is *out of reverence for
Jesus Christ.* Christians need to give thanks to God through
Jesus Christ for what he has done for them, and for what God has
done for them in Christ. All Christians should "*be subject to one
another*". The participle ὑποτασσόμενοι, *hupotassomenoi* being
a present participle does not begin a new sentence but connects
back to the previous thought and should be translated "*being
subject to one another.*"

This pericope introduces a block of material relating to how
Christians should live in both the home and in the church in a
manner that is out of reverence for the Fatherhood of God and
the Lordship of Christ. Discussing the "house rules" regarding
how members of a Christian household should live, Lincoln
points out:

> "5:21–33 can be seen as a unit. Its first verse acts as a
> link. completing the thought of 5:18–20 about being
> filled with the Spirit and at the same time introducing a
> new topic. submission, which is to be developed in the
> rest of the passage. Its introductory function is twofold.
> Not only does the admonition of v 22 depend on the
> participle of v 21 for its sense. but the notion of fear in

the latter verse also provides the opening element of an inclusio which will be completed in v 33."[44]

Careful comparison of several translations, e.g. the NASV, the RSV, and the NIV will reveal that there are several punctuation and paragraphing differences in this text. These differences are indicated in the major Greek New Testaments such as the Kurt Aland et al, and the Nestle Greek New Testaments. The differences do not make any significant change to the meaning of the text, but some do strengthen how one should read this text.

The text of **Eph 5:20, 21** literally reads like this, "*[20]always in everything giving thanks to God the Father at all times in the name of our Lord Jesus, [21]being subject to one another out of reverence for Christ.*" Our submission to one another is out of reverence for Christ, and in thanks to God the Father. The point Paul is making is that there is a theological reason for our submission to one another. We are subject to one another out of reverence for Christ.

In this pericope Paul introduces an interesting and significant sociological and ethical block of material, technically identified by a German term *Haustafeln* which refers to the concept of "house rules" or rules of behavior which are recognized as good sociological citizenry. Cultured and educated Gentiles, Romans and Greeks recognized certain sets of family or house rules for the family in keeping with good society.

Lincoln adds regarding some scholarly opinion of *Haustafeln* that some scholars regarded Paul's use of *Haustafeln* as a continuation of his previous reactions as in 1 Corinthians to excessive behavior relating to women and slaves who believed that because they were in Christ all roles of behavior had been reduced to equality in the church. Note Lincoln's comments:

"More recently, however, it has been argued convincingly, especially by Balch ... that this sort of analysis does not do enough justice to the important

---

[44] Lincoln, *Ephesians*, p. 352 ff; Pater O'Brian, *The Letter to the Ephesians*, Eph 5:18-21.

influence of the discussion about the topic of household management in the ancient world. This discussion, which treats husband-wife, parent-child, and master-slave relationships, focuses on authority and subordination within these relationships, and relates the topic of the household to the larger topic of the state, can be found as early as the classical Greek philosophers ... It is worth noting how Aristotle introduces his discussion of the topic: "Now that it is clear what are the component parts of the state, we have first of all to discuss household management: for every state is composed of households ... [45]

As a demonstration that Christians also hold to a lofty set of house rules and respect for good citizenry Paul encourages Christians to live according to a Christian set of *haustafeln* which were similar to those recognized in Greek and Roman society.

Christians, however, do not do this simply because of cultural norms, although this surely was part of Paul's concern, they do this out of reverence for Christ and in thanksgiving to God the Father. Furthermore, by demonstrating good family life and citizenry they bring glory to God through Christ and the church. Without sociologically recognized sound ethical house behavior Christians would not be able to bring glory to God in their Gentile communities, or to influence Gentiles for Christian consideration.

Eph 5:21. The connecting present participle ὑποτασσόμενοι, *hupotassomenoi* that opens 5:21 means *constantly being subject* or *in submission* (ὑποτάσσω, *hupotásso*). This does not mean degrading or debasing oneself, but implies *being submissive, subjecting oneself,* or *considering the other person first, being subordinate to, being subject to, submitting to, or obeying.*

Since the participle is a present participle it carries the sense of *constantly being subject* to one another! *Out of reverence for Christ* all Christians should *constantly be subject to one another.*

---

[45] Lincoln, *Ephesians*, p. 357.

Friberg and Miller add that the submission is "with a component of voluntary submission (to) *be submissive, obey, subject oneself*".[46]

On *hupotássō, be subject,* Kittel's *Theological Dictionary* adds, "*to place oneself under, the general rule demands readiness to renounce one's own will for the sake of others,* i.e. *agapáō,* and *to give precedence to others.*[47] In keeping with this note Paul's exhortation at Rom 12:9-18, "*live in harmony with all, outdo one another in showing honor*". Thus, in the Christian context, being subject to one another means *out of love putting the other person first.* Delling in Kittle continues his comments on the relationship between submission and lowliness by referring to Eph 4:2, "The demand for mutual submission among Christians shows especially that ὑποτάσσομαι (submission) bears a material relation to Christian ταπεινοφροσύνη (lowliness).[48]

An important point is to note that all Christians out if reverence for Christ and as an example to their neighbors are constantly to be subject or in submission to one another; wives to their husbands (5:22); husbands to their wives (5:25); children to parents (6:1); parents to children (6:4); slaves to masters (6:5); masters to slaves (6:9).

Eph 5:25. The Christian role model for all of this is Christ who, although he was head of the church, so loved the church that he humbled himself (Phil 2:5-8) and gave himself up for the church.

This is a profound point; Christ as the Lord of all creation, the head of the church, submitted himself to the church by giving himself up for the church! Note carefully Phil 2:5-11 regarding *having the mind of Christ and emptying oneself of self, becoming a servant to all*:

---

[46]Friberg, Timothy, Friberg, Barbara, Miller, Neva F. *Analytical Lexicon of the Greek New Testament.* Grand Rapids: Baker Books, 2000.
[47]Gerhard Delling, in Kittel, Gerhard Friedrich, *Theological Dictionary of the New Testament,* 1964/1976. Italics IAF.
[48]Gerhard Delling, Kittel, *Theological Dictionary of the New Testament.*

"Have this mind among yourselves, which is yours in Christ Jesus, [6] *who, though he was in the form of God, did not count equality with God a thing to be grasped,* [7] *but emptied himself, taking the form of a servant, being born in the likeness of men.* [8] *And being found in human form he humbled himself and became obedient unto death, even death on a cross.* [9] *Therefore God has highly exalted him and bestowed on him the name which is above every name,* [10] *that at the name of Jesus every knee should bow, in heaven and on earth and under the earth,* [11] *and every tongue confess that Jesus Christ is Lord, to the glory of God the Father."*

This point is so striking that I simply must re-emphasize it! *Christ, the sovereign Lord of the kingdom and head of the church so loved the church that he gave himself up for the church.* Now that is submission! If Christ can submit himself to the church as a humble servant then Christians surely can submit themselves to one another!

Consider verse 11 in the above quote, *"and every tongue confess that Jesus Christ is Lord, to the glory of God the Father."* Christ certainly is an outstanding model of how to bring glory to God!

The key to this whole Christian *Haustafeln* is Christ's example, and all Christians following him by submitting themselves to one another. Christians do this not as a duty but out of thanksgiving and reverence for Christ!

Compare Paul's similar *Haustafeln* at Col 3:18ff.

At **Eph 5:26, 27** Paul mentions that Christ in his love for the church sanctified and cleansed the church by his blood that the church may be without blemish. Christ's concern for the church was in the best interest of the church, not of himself. The analogy Paul is drawing in this little piece about Christ's love for the church is that this is how the husband should love his wife. *His point is that the husband should always act in the best interest of his wife, not selfishly in his own interest.*

Eph 5:32. Paul sets this whole *Haustafeln* again in a theological context. *"The mystery is a profound one, and I am saying that it refers to Christ and the church, however, let each one of you love his wife as himself, and let the wife see that she respects her husband."* Although starting off with the regular *Haustafeln* Paul comes back to Christ and the church as the ideal model for Christian household and family behavior in the Ephesian or Colossian culture[49].

---

[49] Difficulties arise when one examines Paul's *Haustafeln* and attempts to insert it into contemporary sociological postmodern egalitarian concerns. This is not the place to engage in the complex dialogue between postmodern, complementarian, or egalitarian concerns. However, the fundamental exegetical and theological hermeneutic principles apply. The practice of translating contextually defined texts into contemporary situations involves careful biblical critical exegetical studies of the text, identification of the theological principles involved in the text, then finding contemporary situations in which to apply the theological principles. It does not matter whether one is of a complementarian, moderate complementarian, egalitarian, moderately egalitarian, African tribal, or African matriarchal culture or mindset, the same principle applies; through sound biblical critical exegetical practice seek to identify the theological principles and them apply them to whatever culture or mindset in which one finds oneself. In the case under consideration, the Christian *Haustafeln* outlined by Paul, the fundamental theological principles are to live in the family out of appropriate respect for God and Christ, manifesting love and concern for those in the family. For a brief bibliography on this topic cf. Piper, John, et al. *Discovering Biblical Manhood and Womanhood: A Response to Evangelical Feminism*, Wheaton: Ill.: Crossway, 2002, and Grudem, Wayne, et al, *Biblical Foundations for Manhood and Womanhood*, Wheaton, Ill.: Crossway, 2002 Osborn, Carroll D., Ed. *Essays on Women in Earliest Christianity*, vols. 1 & 2, College Press, 1993, 1995, and *Women in the Church*, ACU Press, 2001.

The Church's Warfare
Eph 6:10-20

"10 Finally, be strong in the Lord and in the strength of his might. 11 Put on the whole armor of God, that you may be able to stand against the wiles of the devil. 12 For we are not contending against flesh and blood, but against the principalities, against the powers, against the world rulers of this present darkness, against the spiritual hosts of wickedness in the heavenly places. 13 Therefore take the whole armor of God, that you may be able to withstand in the evil day, and having done all, to stand. 14 Stand therefore, having girded your loins with truth, and having put on the breastplate of righteousness, 15 and having shod your feet with the equipment of the gospel of peace; 16 besides all these, taking the shield of faith, with which you can quench all the flaming darts of the evil one. 17 And take the helmet of salvation, and the sword of the Spirit, which is the word of God. 18 Pray at all times in the Spirit, with all prayer and supplication. To that end keep alert with all perseverance, making supplication for all the saints, 19 and also for me, that utterance may be given me in opening my mouth boldly to proclaim the mystery of the gospel, 20 for which I am an ambassador in chains; that I may declare it boldly, as I ought to speak."

Remember the Gnostic concept of demiurges surrounding the earth, controlling life. Paul writes to explain that in Christ the Christians need have no fear of *the principalities and powers in the heavenly place*, that is, the Gnostic or any other demon world.

Christians living in Asia in the first century A.D. were well aware of the fact that there are spiritual powers that oppose man. Satan being the chief power!

Paul has stressed that Christ defeated the principalities and powers (the spirit world) at the cross and has delivered Christians from these powers, Eph 1:20-23. At Col 1:13, 14, he wrote *"He has delivered us from the dominion of darkness and transferred us to the kingdom of his beloved Son, [14]in whom we have redemption, the forgiveness of sins."*

However, Paul explains that although Satan has ultimately been defeated at the cross he still carries out a bitter war against the saints. Nevertheless, because of Jesus' victory and power over Satan and all other spiritual powers, Christians can also in Christ defeat Satan in their lives through their faith in God's power.

Note these two great passages:

Rom 8:37ff,

> *"No, in all these things we are more than conquerors through him who loved us. [38]For I am sure that neither death, nor life, nor angels, nor principalities, nor things present, nor things to come, nor powers, [39]nor height, nor depth, nor anything else in all creation, will be able to separate us from the love of God in Christ Jesus our Lord."*

Rev 12:10f,

> *"And I heard a loud voice in heaven, saying, "Now the salvation and the power and the kingdom of our God and the authority of his Christ have come, for the accuser of our brethren has been thrown down, who accuses them day and night before our God. [11]And they have conquered him by the blood of the Lamb and by the word of their testimony, for they loved not their lives even unto death."*

Eph 6:13. The discussion of the armor Christians must wear is characterized by the support system they have in Christ. *God* is the *whole armor* Christians must wear in their warfare with Satan. In the presence of God evil has no power!

God, Christ, and the Holy Spirit are all Christians need in their battle against the demonic powers and Satan himself; they have no need of special intuitive Gnostic type knowledge.

A significant background to this Christian armor would be Isa 11:5 where the Messiah is predicted as being shod with righteousness and faithfulness. *"Righteousness shall be the girdle of his waist, and faithfulness the girdle of his loins"*.

The Christian armor would naturally be figuratively modeled after that of the ever present Roman soldier. Eph 6:14ff:

> *" Stand therefore, having girded your loins with truth, and having put on the breastplate of righteousness, [15] and having shod your feet with the equipment of the gospel of peace; [16] besides all these, taking the shield of faith, with which you can quench all the flaming darts of the evil one. [17] And take the helmet of salvation, and the sword of the Spirit, which is the word of God."*

Eph 6:13. Christians must *stand firm* in their faith in the Lord. The word for *stand, anthístēmi* means *to stand against, to oppose, to resist firmly*.

Eph 6:14. Christians must *gird* themselves *with truth*. *Gird* derives from *perizónnumi, to wrap around*. Figuratively, *girding denotes readiness for activity*. The Christians must be wrapped around with truth and constantly ready for action against *the wiles of the devil*, notably in the presence of Gnostic or other false teaching. False teaching relating to numerous philosophical views was rampant in Ephesus with the dominance of the Artemesian cult, mystery religions, and Gnosticism.

In contrast to the many false and strange views *truth, alétheia, that which is genuine and not false* must surround the Christian life and faith. At Eph 4:11 Paul had referred to the teaching ministry of the church which would build up their faith and ministry and mature them in Christ. Truth is simply that which is genuine and the opposite of fiction or myth.

In the context of Ephesians *truth* would represent *that which is true about Jesus* in contrast to the Gnostic denial that the Christ had come in the flesh. Furthermore, it would strengthen the point that all Christians need to combat Satan and the principalities in heavenly places was the correct knowledge of Jesus. Remember, Paul had prayed for them at Eph 1:16ff:

> *" I do not cease to give thanks for you, remembering you in my prayers, [17] that the God of our Lord Jesus Christ,*

the Father of glory, may give you a spirit of wisdom and of revelation in the knowledge of him, [18] having the eyes of your hearts enlightened, that you may know what is the hope to which he has called you, what are the riches of his glorious inheritance in the saints, [19] and what is the immeasurable greatness of his power in us who believe, according to the working of his great might [20] which he accomplished in Christ when he raised him from the dead and made him sit at his right hand in the heavenly places, [21] far above all rule and authority and power and dominion, and above every name that is named, not only in this age but also in that which is to come; [22] and he has put all things under his feet and has made him the head over all things for the church, [23] which is his body, the fulness of him who fills all in all."

Eph 6:15. The footwear of the Christian soldier should be *the gospel of peace.* The good news, the gospel and truth regarding Jesus is all the knowledge Christians need. The gospel message speaks of the good news about Jesus as bringing peace. Cf Rom 5:1, *"Therefore, since we are justified by faith, we have peace with God through our Lord Jesus Christ."*

Eph 6:17. The *helmet of salvation* is the safety and security Christians enjoy knowing they are saved. They also have *the sword of the Spirit which is the word of God.* Christians need no other knowledge to defend themselves from the demonic world than what they already have, *the knowledge of Jesus.*

Christians should remember that in his temptation Jesus leaned on scripture, *"It is written…"* (Matt 4:4, 7). Correct knowledge of God and Jesus as revealed in scripture is essential in the Christian's defense against temptation.

The Christian's armor is thus comprised of *faith, righteousness* (a proper relationship with God), their *knowledge of God and Jesus*, and the fact that *they have already been saved by God in Jesus.*

Eph 4:18. Christians should also draw on the power of prayer. Cf. **Phil 4:6, 7.**

"The Lord is at hand. ⁶Have no anxiety about anything, but in everything by prayer and supplication with thanksgiving let your requests be made known to God. ⁷And the peace of God, which passes all understanding, will keep your hearts and your minds in Christ Jesus."

Eph 6:19, 20. Paul encourages the Ephesians to continue to pray for him that he may have openings to preach and to speak boldly in witness for Jesus. He reminds them that he is still a prisoner "in chains" yet is as such an *ambassador for Christ*.

Major Lessons to Learn from Eph 5:21-6:20:

- Paul has drawn an analogy to the typical *haustafeln* common to most cultured societies in ancient times. It is important that Christians demonstrate to their neighbors that they know how to live good moral lives.
- A basic reason for this moral code and behavior is to provide Christians with an opportunity to bring glory to God in their communities.
- However, Paul adds a major theological ingredient. They live model lives *out of reverence for God and Christ*.
- *All Christians* must learn *to be subject to one another*, husbands to wives and children, wives to husbands, children to parents, slaves to master, and masters to slaves.
- Christians must realize that they are engaged in a spiritual war with Satan and the spiritual principalities and powers in heavenly places.
- Christians must wear the whole armor of God which primarily is God himself. They must clothe themselves with God. In addition there are several other pieces of spiritual armor such as *truth, faith, salvation, the gospel*, and *prayer*. Christians must wrap themselves in the whole armor of God, that is, they must draw on every form of divine and spiritual help in their battle against the wiles of the devil.

Discussion Questions

- Why should Christians be concerned about their moral behavior? Remember first the theological purpose Paul lists in the *Laudatio* of Ephesians. To what are the Christians called and destined to live?
- What is the guiding principle behind the Christian *Haustafeln* mentioned by Paul? How should this guide or govern their moral behavior?
- Give some practical situations where the principles of the *Haustafeln* of Ephesians would apply in life today?
- How have we most often abused the principles of the *Haustafeln*? We are not speaking of how others have done this, but of how we do this!
- What does submission mean in the context of living out of reverence of Christ?
- What does it mean to be in submission to one another?
- How can we practice this in the home and in the church?

Lesson 12

Ephesians 6:21-24

The Conclusion of Ephesians

²¹Now that you also may know how I am and what I am doing, Tychicus the beloved brother and faithful minister in the Lord will tell you everything. ²² I have sent him to you for this very purpose, that you may know how we are, and that he may encourage your hearts. ²³ Peace be to the brethren, and love with faith, from God the Father and the Lord Jesus Christ. ²⁴ Grace be with all who love our Lord Jesus Christ with love undying."

Tychicus was Paul's secretary (*amanuenses, scribe*) who was carrying this letter to Ephesus and the surrounding churches. He was also Paul's beloved brother and a faithful minister. He is also mentioned in Col 4:7 as Paul's beloved brother and faithful minister. Paul explains that Tychicus would inform the Christians of Paul's welfare and future plans.

The letter closes with Paul's typical Christian greetings and farewell words. These emphasize the significant and meaningful Christian concepts, *peace, love, and grace.* Paul's use of these three concepts is in the form of a prayer for the Christians.

Peace be to the brethren (*eiréné, inner spiritual peace and tranquility, the cessation of anxiety and tribulation*).

Love with faith from God and Jesus (*agápē, the desire for the very best for the other person or persons*).

Grace for those who love the Lord Jesus Christ (*cháris, favor from God and Jesus Christ*).

Love undying (*aphtharsía, without corruption!*)

Concluding Thoughts from Ephesians

This is a thoughtful letter from Paul who had been for several years involved in missionary evangelism in Asia during the period he was resident in Ephesus (Acts 19). He understood well the challenges faced by the Christians in that region..

Ephesus was a major city in Asia, not the capital of the Roman province, but a major sea port and the religious and intellectual center of Asia. Ephesus had been and would continue to be a major center of mission activity in the Roman Worlds of Asia and Macedonia.

The Ephesian church in the years following Paul's ministry there became the stronghold of Christianity in the region and more books in our New Testament were written for, in, and about the city of Ephesus than any other place.

In later years Timothy ministered in Ephesus (1 and 2 Timothy), as did the Apostle John (The Gospel of John, 1, 2, 3 John, Revelation).

Several religious movements were prominent in Ephesus. The Temple of Artemis (immorality), the Mystery Religions, the Worship of Bacchus (the God of wine), and Gnosticism. All these formed the cultural background behind Paul's concern for the church in Ephesus and the surrounding region.

One should remember the dominance of spiritual powers (Gnosticism and other similar views) in the thinking of the residents of Asia. Likewise Christians should remember the theology of Ephesians is built around the called destiny of Christians to so live their lives that they bring glory to God through Jesus Christ and the church.

Being *in Christ* is a major theological theme to this epistle.

Notice the flow of thought in the paranetic sections of Ephesians: The Unity of Jews and Gentiles in the church, the moral life of the Christians, the conduct and example of the Christian family in society, the war with spiritual powers and Satan and the strength of being in Christ in this battle.

Overall the Christians should draw on the *strengthening power of the indwelling Holy Spirit* in their lives of Christians living.

Christians must seek the right kind of knowledge which is centered on the knowledge of Jesus Christ applied with spiritual wisdom and understanding.

Discussion Questions

- First, discuss the major theological theme for this study of Ephesians and what it means to you.
- What other major encouraging lessons can we learn from Eph 1:3-14?
- List these and discuss how they can be an encouragement in your life.
- When did God decide we could be his children in Christ?
- What does this mean to you today? Be practical!
- What do you think of Biblical Predestination? How is it different from Calvinistic Predestination, and how does Biblical Predestination work?
- What kind of unity is *ontological* unity and how does it come about (Eph 4:3), and what is *cognitive* unity and how does it come about (Eph 4:12-16)?
- What should an understanding of the two kinds of unity do for us in the church today? Notice particularly and comment on Rom 14:1-15:7.
- How should the church manifest the mystery of God and the wisdom of God to the world today (Eph 3:9, 10)? Keep your answers or discussion in the context of this text.
- What is the theological basis of Christian family life (Eph 5:21)?
- What is the overriding principle of submission (Eph 5:20, 21)?
- Discuss ways in which this would apply to us today.

Lesson 5a
A Brief Excursus on Pauline and Calvinistic Predestination

Rom 8:28-31 and Eph 1:3-12

Bibliography

Barrett, C. K., *The Epistle to the Romans*, Peabody, Mass.: Hendriksen, 1991.

Bauer, Walter, William F. Arndt, and F. Wilber Gingrich, *A Greek English Lexicon of the New Testament*, Chicago: University of Chicago.

Bloesch, Donald G. *Essentials of Evangelical Theology*, Vol. 2, New York, Harper and Row, 1982.

Dunn, R. D. G., *Romans 1-8*, Dallas: Word Books, 1998.

Fair, Ian A., *Wolfhart Pannenberg's Reaction to Dialectical Theology*, PhD dissertation, University of KwaZulu-Natal, 1975.

Fitzmyer, Joseph A., *Romans*, The Anchor Bible, New York: Doubleday, 1993.

Guthrie, Donald, *New Testament Theology*, Downers Grove: IVP, 1981.

Käsemann, Ernst, *Commentary on Romans*, Grand Rapids: William B. Eerdmans, 1980.

Kittel, Gerhard, *Theological Dictionary of the New Testament*, Gerhard Kittel, G. W. Bromiley, and G. Friedrich, Eds., 1964.

Michel, Otto, Οἰκονομία, *Theological Dictionary of the New Testament*, Gerhard Kittel, G. W. Bromiley, and G. Friedrich, Eds., 1964.

Mounce, Robert H., *Romans*, Nashville: Broadman and Holman, 1995.

Newman, Barkly M. and Eugene A. Nida, *Romans, A Translator's Handbook*, New York: United Bible Societies, 1973.

Pannenberg, Wolfhart, *Basic Questions and Answers*, Vol. 2, Philadelphia; Fortress Press, 1971.

Pannenberg, Wolfhart, *Jesus, God, and Man*, London: SCM Press, 1968.

Richardson, Alan, *A Dictionary of Christian Theology*, London: SCM Press, 1969.

Schmidt, K. L., Προορίζω, *Theological Dictionary of the New Testament*. Gerhard Kittel, G., W. Bromiley, and G. Friedrich, Eds., Grand Rapids: Eerdmans, 1964.

Schreiner, Thomas R., *Romans*, Grand Rapids, Baker Books, 1998.

The Anchor Bible Dictionary, David Noel Freedman, Ed., New York: Doubleday, 1992.

Tupper, E. Frank, *The Theology of Wolfhart Pannenberg*, Philadelphia; The Westminster Press, 1972, pp. 122 ff.

Zodhiates, Spiros, *The Complete Word Study Dictionary: New Testament*. Chattanooga: AMG Publishers, 2000.

Introduction

We encounter the biblical doctrine of predestination primarily in Paul at Eph 1:3-12 and Rom 8:28, 29. Predestination is a biblical topic and doctrine. Although Paul makes considerable use of the principle of predestination his views are vastly different from Calvinistic Predestination.

This study does not portend to be an exhaustive study of Calvinistic Predestination. Our purpose will be to pursue what Paul has to say about predestination and then briefly compare this with Calvinistic Predestination.

Predestination in Paul's theology is closely tied to God's *foreknowledge* and a *plan* that God *determined before the foundation of the world*, not to some arbitrary choice God makes as to who will be saved and who lost!

We will examine the two texts in which Paul discusses *predestination* (προορίζω *proorízō*), the *foreknowledge* (προγινώσκω *proginṓskō*), and God *destining* (προορίζω *proorizō*) something to happen in the future (Eph 1:5, 12, and Rom 8:29, 30) long before he created the world and man.

There are several other texts that make statements regarding God's predetermined actions or knowledge; for example, Acts 1:23; 4:28; 1 Cor 2:7. We will first examine the two major Pauline texts in which we find biblical predestination being developed and then consider Acts 1:23; 4:28; and 1 Cor 2:7.

As always, it is imperative that we consider these texts in their immediate biblical and theological context to get the flow of thought Paul was making.

Eph 1:3-12:

> "Blessed be the God and Father of our Lord Jesus Christ, who has blessed us in Christ with every spiritual blessing in the heavenly places, *4* even as he chose us in him before the foundation of the world, that we should be holy and blameless before him. *5* He destined us in love to be his sons through Jesus Christ, according to the purpose of his will, *6* to the praise of his glorious grace which he freely bestowed on us in the Beloved. *7* In him we have redemption through his blood, the forgiveness of our trespasses, according to the riches of his grace *8* which he lavished upon us. *9* For he has made known to us in all wisdom and insight the mystery of his will, according to his purpose which he set forth in Christ *10* as a plan for the fulness of time, to unite all things in him, things in heaven and things on earth. *11* In him, according to the purpose of him who accomplishes all things according to the counsel of his will, *12* we who first hoped in Christ have been destined and appointed to live for the praise of his glory."

Rom 8: 29, 30:

"We know that in everything God works for good with those who love him, who are called according to his purpose. 29 For those whom he foreknew he also predestined to be conformed to the image of his Son, in order that he might be the first-born among many brethren. 30 And those whom he predestined he also called; and those whom he called he also justified; and those whom he justified he also glorified."

We will note below that a better translation of this initial text reads, "We know that everything works for good for those who love God ..."

Acts 2:23:

"this Jesus, delivered up according to the definite plan and foreknowledge of God, you crucified and killed by the hands of lawless men ..."

Acts 4:28:

"The kings of the earth set themselves in array, and the rulers were gathered together, against the Lord and against his Anointed'—²⁷ for truly in this city there were gathered together against thy holy servant Jesus, whom thou didst anoint, both Herod and Pontius Pilate, with the Gentiles and the peoples of Israel, ²⁸ to do whatever thy hand and thy plan had predestined to take place."

1 Cor 2:7:

"But we impart a secret and hidden wisdom of God, which God decreed before the ages for our glorification."

Brief Study of the Word Group Surrounding "Predestined"

Προγινώσκω, Προορίζω, Οἰκονομία

Προγινώσκω, *proginōskō, to know beforehand.* Spiros Zodhiates comments regarding προγινώσκω:

"Προέγνω, προγινώσκω, proginōskō, means "to know before. To perceive or recognize beforehand, know previously, take into account or specially consider beforehand, to grant prior acknowledgement or recognition to someone, to foreknow ... Used of God's eternal counsel it includes all that He has considered and purposed to do prior to human history. In the language of Scripture, something foreknown is not simply that which God was aware of prior to a certain point. Rather, it is presented as that which God gave prior consent to, that which received His favorable or special recognition. Hence, this term is reserved for those matters which God favorably, deliberately and freely chose and ordained."[50]

Several commentators observe that the Old Testament background to the use of God's *foreknowledge* as in the Hebrew behind the Septuagint (LXX) is *yāda. Yāda,* it is maintained, was used in reference to the covenantal love in which God sets his affection on those who he has foreknows and has chosen.[51] Thus, we see in the use of *foreknew,* a reference to those who are in a covenant relationship with God, which in the context of Paul's discussion in Romans refers to those in a righteous relationship with God based on faith in God or in Jesus. The Hebrew concept of *election* based on the *foreknowledge* of God and *covenantal faith* is evident in Paul's use of *foreknowledge* in this periscope, Rom 8:26-30.

Προορίζω, *prooridzō,* regarding προορίζω, *prooridzō, to destine or predestine,* Spiros Zodhiates observes, "Προορίζω, *proorízō;* derives from *pró, before,* and *horízō, to determine.* Προορίζω, *proorízō* thus means *to determine or decree beforehand."*[52]

K. L. Schmidt in Kittle's *Theological Dictionary of the New Testament* on προορίζω notes that:

---

[50] Spiros Zodhiates, *The Complete Word Study Dictionary: New Testament.* Chattanooga: AMG Publishers, 2000.

[51] Cf. for instance Thomas R Schreiner, *Romans*, Grand Rapids: Baker Books, 1998, p. 452, and other similar references in Fitzmyer, et al.

[52] Spiros Zodhiates, *The Complete Word Study Dictionary: New Testament.* Chattanooga: AMG Publishers, 2000.

"This comparatively rare and late word is used in the Gk. Bible only 6 times in the NT in the sense "to foreordain," "to predestinate." Since God is eternal and has ordained everything before time. προορίζειν is a stronger form of ὁρίζειν … The synonyms and textual history show that the ref. in προγινώσκειν is the same. R. 8:29: οὓς προέγνω, καὶ προώρισεν συμμόρφους τῆς εἰκόνος τοῦ υἱοῦ αὐτοῦ, R. 8:30: οὓς … προώρισεν … The omniscient God has determined everything in advance. both persons and things in salvation history, with Jesus Christ as the goal. When Herod and Pilate work together with the Gentiles and the mob against Jesus Christ. it may be said: ἡ χείρ σου (God's) καὶ ἡ βουλὴ προώρισεν γενέσθαι. Ac. 4:28. Herein lies the hidden wisdom of God in a mystery, ἣν προώρισεν ὁ θεὸς πρὸ τῶν αἰώνων εἰς δόξαν ἡμῶν, 1 C. 2:7, → IV, 819. *The goal of our predestination is divine sonship through Jesus Christ* …"[53]

Bauer, Arndt and Gingrich, and Danker in the Arndt and Gingrich *Greek-English Lexicon of the Greek New Testament* state that προορίζω, *proorízō*, means "to *decide upon beforehand, predestine.*"[54]

Spiros Zodhiates in his *Complete Word Study Dictionary* observes:

"Πρόθεσις *próthesis*; to purpose or plan … setting forth. presentation, an exposition, determination, plan, or will. It involves purpose, resolve, and design. A placing in view or openly displaying something."[55]

Οἰκονομία, *oikonomía, to plan.* Regarding the *plan*, οἰκονομία, *oikonomía,* which God has had since the foundation

---

[53] K. L. Schmidt in Kittel, G., Bromiley, G. W., & Friedrich, G., Eds., *Theological Dictionary of the New Testament*. Grand Rapids: Eerdmans, 1964. I have italicized last sentence for emphasis, IAF.
[54] Walter Bauer, William F. Arndt, F. Wilber Gingrich, *A Greek English Lexicon of the New Testament*, Chicago: University of Chicago.
[55] Spiros Zodhiates, The Complete Word Study Dictionary: New Testament.

of the world, Spiros Zodhiates states that this is the kind of plan that the manager of a household would have regarding the management of his estate:

"Οἰκονομία. oikonomía ... from oikonoméō ... to be a manager of a household. The position, work, responsibility or arrangement of an administration, as of a house or of property, either one's own or another's (Luke 16:2; Sept.: Is. 22:19); a spiritual dispensation, management, or economy (1 Cor. 9:17; Eph. 1:10; 3:2; Col. 1:25). The "dispensation of God" means the administration of divine grace."[56]

Otto Michel in Kittel's *Theological Dictionary* writes:

"In the NT οἰκονομία first means ... the office of household administration and the discharge of this office ... Paul uses the term for the apostolic office, 1 C. 9:17: οἰκονομίαν πεπίστευμαι. He is entrusted with an office; he does not preach the Gospel of his own accord; he does what he has to do, cf. 1 Th. 2:4: δεδοκιμάσμεθα ὑπὸ τοῦ θεοῦ πιστευθῆναι τὸ εὐαγγέλιον. The word also occurs, with paraphrases and embellishments, in the Prison Letters: Col. 1:25: κατὰ τὴν οἰκονομίαν τοῦ θεοῦ τὴν δοθεῖσάν μοι εἰς ὑμᾶς, according to the divine office towards you with which God has commissioned me; Eph. 3:2: τὴν οἰκονομίαν τῆς χάριτος τοῦ θεοῦ τῆς δοθείσης μοι εἰς ὑμᾶς, you have heard of the office of divine grace which has been laid upon me in service towards you. A distinctive feature in these epistles is that there is room for doubt whether οἰκονομία denotes office or the divine plan of salvation; the two are closely linked in the Prison Letters ... The word also means "plan of salvation," "administration of salvation," "order of salvation." In this sense it has both a religious and a general significance ... In Eph. 1:10 the reference is to God's plan of salvation which He has undertaken to execute in the fulness of

---

[56] Spiros Zodhiates, The Complete Word Study Dictionary: New Testament

times (εἰς οἰκονομίαν τοῦ πληρώματος τῶν καιρῶν). Eph. 3:9 also refers to the actualising of the mystery which was hidden in God, the Creator of all things, before the times (τίς ἡ οἰκονομία τοῦ μυστηρίου τοῦ ἀποκεκρυμμένου ἀπὸ τῶν αἰώνων ἐν τῷ θεῷ τῷ τὰ πάντα κτίσαντι).[57]

Brief Exegesis of Eph 1:3-12

Predestined to Bring Glory to God in Christ!

In the following quote from Eph 1:3-12 I have intentionally italicized in bold certain expressions for emphasis since they are profoundly important to our discussion.

> *"Blessed be the God and Father of our Lord Jesus Christ, who has **blessed us in Christ** with every spiritual blessing in the heavenly places, [4] even as **he chose us in him before the foundation of the world** (God's corporate election in Christ according to his foreknowledge), that we should be holy and blameless before him. [5] He **destined** (προορίζω, proorízō, predestined, decided, or determined beforehand) us in love to be his sons through Jesus Christ (a corporate not individual purpose), according to the purpose of his will, [6] to the praise of his glorious grace which he freely bestowed on us in the Beloved. [7] **In him** (corporately in Christ) we have redemption through his blood, the forgiveness of our trespasses, according to the riches of his grace [8] which he lavished upon us. [9] For he has made known to us in all wisdom and insight the mystery of his will, according to **his purpose which he set forth in Christ** [10] as a **plan** (οἰκονομία, oikonomia, economy, plan, system) for the fulness of time (an eschatological plan) to unite all things in him, things in heaven and things on earth. [11] **In him** (corporately), according to the*

---

[57]Otto Michel, Οἰκονομία, in Kittel, *Theological Dictionary of the New Testament*, Gerhard Kittel, G. W. Bromiley, and G. Friedrich, Eds., 1964.

purpose (πρόθεσις, próthesis, determined plan) of him
who accomplishes all things according to the counsel of
his will, [12] *we who first hoped in Christ have been*
destined *(προορίζω, proorizō, predestined, decided, or*
determined) and appointed to live for the praise of his
glory."

This text is extremely important to any understanding of predestination: Several points stand out from this text. *God knew what he was* doing when he planned his creation; creation did not happen serendipitously, or by accident!

God had a plan to save or redeem man and his creation even before he created the world and man! Before creation God *destined* or *predestined* man's salvation, that is, *he had a plan to save or redeem fallen man in Jesus Christ*. Paul argues later in Ephesians that fallen man is saved by God's grace through faith *corporately in Jesus Christ.*

Eph 1:3. "*Blessed be the God and Father of our Lord Jesus Christ, who has blessed us in Christ with every spiritual blessing in the heavenly plac*es …" Paul affirms that it is *in Christ* that we have every spiritual blessing. In the Gnostic or pagan environment this is an extremely important point. There is nothing the Gnostic Redeemer could add that man needs that God has not already provided for in Christ Jesus! God has already provided every spiritual blessing man needs and this is found in Christ and not in some esoteric secret knowledge. To this Paul adds **Eph 2:1-8**;

"And you he made alive, when you were dead through
the trespasses and sins [2] *in which you once walked,*
following the course of this world, following the prince of
the power of the air, the spirit that is now at work in the
sons of disobedience. [3] *Among these we all once lived in*
the passions of our flesh, following the desires of body
and mind, and so we were by nature children of wrath,
like the rest of mankind. [4] *But God, who is rich in mercy,*
out of the great love with which he loved us, [5] *even when*
we were dead through our trespasses, made us alive

together with Christ (by grace you have been saved), *[6] and raised us up with him, and made us sit with him in the heavenly places in Christ Jesus, [7] that in the coming ages he might show the immeasurable riches of his grace in kindness toward us in Christ Jesus. [8] For by grace you have been saved through faith; and this is not your own doing, it is the gift of God— [9] not because of works, lest any man should boast. [10] For we are his workmanship, created in Christ Jesus for good works, which God prepared beforehand, that we should walk in them."*

God's plan was predetermined (predestined) according to his foreknowledge as a *corporate* plan. Man would not be saved in view of personal traits or works! It is only **in Christ** that man would be saved. God planned, destined, decided before creation that *those corporately in the body Christ* would be saved and bring glory to himself.

The lengthy pericope, **Eph 1:3-12** thus speaks of *corporate predestination in Christ*, not private personal or Calvinistic arbitrary predestination!

Fallen man decides for himself after hearing the gospel message whether to believe it and be saved by and *in Christ, or not to* believe it! *Man has the freedom to believe or not to believe!* Man's coming to faith or rejection of faith in Christ is not an arbitrary predetermined choice of God. It is fully within man's freedom to make this decision to have faith. If not, then all of the calls on men in Scripture to believe mean nothing!

At **Rom 10:14-16** Paul asks a perceptive question,

"But how are men to call upon him in whom they have not believed? And how are they to believe in him of whom they have never heard? And how are they to hear without a preacher? [15] And how can men preach unless they are sent? As it is written, "How beautiful are the feet of those who preach good news!" [16] But they have not all obeyed the gospel; for Isaiah says, "Lord, who has believed what he has heard from us?" [17] So faith comes from what is

heard, and what is heard comes by the preaching of Christ."

Salvation is the result of God's *predetermined grace* (*by grace he determined before time*) to send Jesus to die on the cross. Note the interesting statement by John in Revelation regarding Jesus' death. Rev 13:8. The NIV translation of this verse is more in keeping with the Greek text which unfortunately the RSV has translated to be parallel to another similar expression regarding the book of life rather than a precise translation of the Greek. The NIV reads;

"All inhabitants of the earth will worship the beast—all whose names have not been written in the book of life belonging to *the Lamb that was slain from the creation of the world.*"

The point is that according to John and Revelation God had decided *before the foundation of the world that Jesus would die for fallen man.* We should note that Rev 13:8 is a theological observation; not an historical statement!

Likewise Jesus' resurrection was not an afterthought but a predetermined plan. This predetermined plan of God lay at the root of Peter's great Pentecost sermon at Acts 2. Cf 2:23ff.

"[22]*Men of Israel, hear these words: Jesus of Nazareth, a man attested to you by God with mighty works and wonders and signs which God did through him in your midst, as you yourselves know——*[23] *this Jesus, delivered up according to the definite plan and foreknowledge of God, you crucified and killed by the hands of lawless men.* [24] *But God raised him up, having loosed the pangs of death, because it was not possible for him to be held by it."*

Before creation God had planned for Jesus death and resurrection and it was God's predetermined power to raise Jesus from the dead. Jesus' resurrection was not a spur of the moment decision by God forced on him by the death of Jesus. Like Jesus' death his resurrection had been predetermined by God as part of his eternal plan to redeem man. Paul explained to the

Corinthian church that the death, burial, and resurrection was a primary and central fact of the gospel proclamation, 1 Cor 15:1-5:

> "Now I would remind you, brethren, in what terms I preached to you the gospel, which you received, in which you stand, [2] by which you are saved, if you hold it fast— unless you believed in vain. [3] For I delivered to you as of first importance what I also received, that Christ died for our sins in accordance with the scriptures, [4] that he was buried, that he was raised on the third day in accordance with the scriptures ..."

In contrast to the gospel call for everyone to believe, repent, and be baptized, Calvinistic Predestination holds that Jesus died only for those who God had predetermined would be saved and not for all fallen men! I like Peter's response the Jews on the day of Pentecost when they asked what they needed to do after believing in the death and resurrection of Jesus, "Repent, and be baptized *every one of you* in the name of Jesus Christ for the forgiveness of your sins; and you shall receive the gift of the Holy Spirit" Acts 2:38.

According to Calvinistic predestination this call of Peter's to the Jews for everyone to repent does not make sense! According to Calvinistic predestination the gospel call is *not for everyone*, only for those predestined to salvation! We will examine this further shortly.

John, however, in his Gospel wrote;

> "For God so loved the world that he gave his only Son, that whoever believes in him should not perish but have eternal life. [17] For God sent the Son into the world, not to condemn the world, but that the world might be saved through him. [18] He who believes in him is not condemned; he who does not believe is condemned already, because he has not believed in the name of the only Son of God." John 3:16-18.

Sounds to me like God was offering salvation to all the world if they would believe in Jesus!

There is a strong *proleptic eschatological* emphasis in God's predestined plan, (a *proleptic[58] inaugurated and final end time plan*). God's predestined eternal plan which will be fulfilled finally at the end of time is *being received in advance of the end through the faith of believers and not by an arbitrary predestined decision of God that some should be saved*! God's plan was conceived before time began to be fulfilled (inaugurated eschatology – the end has already begun) in history in Christ and ultimately to be full realized at *the end of time*, at the general resurrection and final judgment. Note Paul's comment at Eph 1:9, 10:

> *"For he has made known to us in all wisdom and insight the mystery of his will, according to his purpose which he set forth in Christ [10]as a plan (οἰκονομία, oikonomia, economy, plan, system) for the fulness of time (an eschatological plan) to unite all things in him, things in heaven and things on earth."*

The point to be stressed in Eph 1:3-10 is that man's salvation and redemption was *predetermined* or *predestined in God's plan to be fulfilled in Christ by those who would believe in Jesus and God's plan*. Paul was not saying that individuals are predestined to be saved only that *they were predestined to be saved corporately in Christ*. Simply put, Paul is saying that *God had decided before creation to save people in Christ*.

A point not to be overlooked is that according to God's predestined plan those in Christ were predestined to bring glory to God! Eph 1:11, 12;

> *[11]In him, according to the purpose of him who accomplishes all things according to the counsel of his will, [12]we who first hoped in Christ have been destined and appointed to live for the praise of his glory."*

---

[58] This is a theological term which implies that we are receiving something in advance of the end. *Proleptic* derives from a Latin word and two Greek words, the Latin *prolēpsis*, and the Greek, from *prolambanein, to anticipate before*. It announces that something is received before its fulfillment.

Brief Exegesis of Rom 8:29, 30

Predestined to be Conformed to the Image of His Son!

Paul also addressed God's predetermined plan in a powerful text in which he was reassuring the Romans of the decisiveness of their redemption. Rom 8: 29, 30 reads;

> *"We know that in everything God works for good with those who love him, who are called according to his purpose. [29] For those whom he foreknew he also predestined to be conformed to the image of his Son, in order that he might be the first-born among many brethren. [30] And those whom he predestined he also called; and those whom he called he also justified; and those whom he justified he also glorified."*

First, Rom 8:28 is a notoriously difficult text to translate! The Greek reads "οἴδαμεν δὲ ὅτι τοῖς ἀγαπῶσιν τὸν θεὸν πάντα συνεργεῖ εἰς ἀγαθόν, τοῖς κατὰ πρόθεσιν κλητοῖς οὖσιν." Translated *literally* this reads "Now we know for the ones loving God all things work together for good, for those being called according to purpose." The passage is complicated in that there is no subject/nominative noun (Θεός, *Theós*, God) in the better manuscripts to the verb συνεργεῖ, *is working*, but Θεός is found as a subject/nominative in some good manuscripts[59]. Should we read that *God works all things for good* (RSV) or simply that *all things work together for good* for those who love God (NIV, NRSV)? The better manuscripts support the last reading, as do Fitzmyer, Schreiner, Barrett, Dunn, and Käsemann[60]! But on its own this latter translation still raises problems! Do all things simply work together for all kinds of good for those who love God? How can this be and what does *good* mean?

---

[59] Bruce M. Metzger in *A Textual Commentary on the Greek New Testament*, United Bible Society, 1994 on Rom 8:28 observes that the committee working on this text "deemed" the evidence for including Θεός, *Theos* to be "too narrowly supported to be admitted into the text."
[60] Cf. The bibliography above for these authors.

Second, how do we understand ἀγαθόν, *good*! In the Jewish context it usually meant *spiritual good*, not necessarily all kinds of good. Most scholarly commentators observe that what Paul has in mind with his reference to *good* is the *ultimate eschatological good* that comes at *the end of time*, especially in the general resurrection of the saints to glory with Christ.[61]

When this text is considered in its Pauline Romans context of suffering, the prayers which Christians have difficulty expressing and in which the Holy Spirit assists, and in the real context of Christians ultimately being more than conquerors in Christ, then the eschatological end time *hope* and *good* defines everything working for *the ultimate eschatological good of those who love God*.

Thus in this somewhat complicated text we see Paul assuring Christians in the context of their weakness, hardship, and suffering (Rom 8:26) that all things will ultimately work out for the good of those who love God and do not lose their faith. He then moves on to explain that the Christian's salvation and future is sure since it has been *predetermined* by God in Christ. Those whom he foresaw he predestined to be saved and glorified in Christ. We should remember that at Eph 1:11 Paul had assured the Ephesians that God is capable of accomplishing his purpose and predetermined plan. Note Rom 8:37-39:

> [37] *No, in all these things we are more than conquerors through him who loved us.* [38] *For I am sure that neither death, nor life, nor angels, nor principalities, nor things present, nor things to come, nor powers,* [39] *nor height, nor depth, nor anything else in all creation, will be able to separate us from the love of God in Christ Jesus our Lord.*

If we see Rom 8:28 as a transitional verse between the Holy Spirit interceding for us and God having predestined us to be conformed to the image of his Son, the Jewish spiritual sense of

---

[61] Cf. Joseph A. Fitzmyer; Ernst Käsemann; Thomas R. Schreiner; R. D. G. Dunn in the bibliography.

ultimate good seems more appropriate to the context. Joseph A. Fitzmyer observes:

> *"The overall context of this pericope is that nothing in this life can harm Christians, whether it be suffering or the attack of hostile evil powers, for all of these can contribute to the destiny to which Christians are called, and they are now referred to as 'those who love God'."*[62]

Joseph Fitzmyer also has a few other significant statements regarding Rom 8:29:

> "One encounters in these verses the first mention of "predestination," which Paul will again mention in chap. 9. The combination of Pauline verses on the topic in these chapters led to a preoccupation with them in predestinarian controversies of later centuries. What Paul asserts here in this regard is stated from a corporate point of view. He does not have in mind the predestination of individuals (either to glory or damnation)."[63]

J. D. G. Dunn adds significantly to the interpretation of this text:

> "Paul assumes that his readers will have in mind the continuity of thought from the previous verses in which human suffering and creation's travail have been integrated. *The assurance that he offers his readers here then is that the experience of human contradiction in which they share as believers is no cause for despair, because God is also God of creation; his purpose for believers is also his purpose for creation and works through creation. His people therefore can be confident that their place within God's purpose is basically in harmony with the unfolding history of creation.* (Italics IAF) Those who love God are those who have acknowledged their creatureliness and let that fact shape their living. Their confidence is in God who is both

---

[62] Joseph A. Fitzmyer, *Romans*, The Anchor Bible Commentary, New York Doubleday, 1992, Rom 8:26-39.
[63] Joseph A. Fitzmyer, *Romans*.

Creator and Father. Just as believers can still pray even when their prayer is marked by complaint and irritation or the complete frustration of speechlessness, so they can still trust even when their sense of alienation and contradiction is at its sharpest, the sense of complete helplessness in the face of nameless forces. They can draw on the assurance that the Spirit who is active in these very frustrations and groanings is active also in these dark providences to bring about good—that is, presumably, for Paul, in helping forward the maturing of the believer (cf. 5:4) and the mortification of the deeds of the body (8:13) ... But in fact, the idea of loving God is untypical of Greco-Roman religiosity, while being characteristically Jewish. Paul therefore draws the vaguer hope of all religious piety within the circle of the more distinctive Jewish faith in the one God. The vaguer, more speculative piety of Greco-Roman religiosity is given clearer definition and more substantial foundation in the Jewish trust in God as Creator and Father ... Having hidden nothing of the contradiction and temptation in which believers find themselves, Paul rounds off his discussion of what God's righteousness means for believers in the harsh reality of daily existence, by voicing his firm certainty that God's will stands over all, in control of all, and that his purpose to bring his creation and creatures to their full intended potential is undefeatable. The goal he purposed for his people was formulated in the mists of time, effected by his own summons, to bring his human creation back into fullness of relation with himself, owned by him and sustained by him and given to share in his splendor. In the full assurance of faith Paul sets aside all the "ifs" and "buts," the qualifications and warnings of the previous three chapters, and affirms the certainty of God fulfilling his purpose of creation and salvation in the tense of action already completed ... The goal of the creator-savior is expressed in terms of the original creation transposed into eschatological mode, as Paul could expect his readers to recognize. It is a transforming of believing man back into the image of God which disobedient man lost.[64]

Furthermore Robert H. Mounce astutely adds that this verse does not address the salvation of the individual but their transformation into the likeness of Jesus;

> "In the present context predestination is not concerned with election to salvation. Rather, God has foreordained that believers be brought into "moral conformity to the likeness of his Son." *What is predestined is that we become like Christ* (cf. 2 Cor 3:18).[65]

What we find in Rom 8:29, 30 is a creative poetic use of a string of aorist verbs! Paul writes;

> *"For those whom he foreknew he also predestined to be conformed to the image of his Son, in order that he might be the first-born among many brethren. [30] And those whom he predestined he also called; and those whom he called he also justified; and those whom he justified he also glorified."*

Käsemann and others point to the unique and purposeful collection of aorist verbs Paul has strung together in this text. The aorist indicative verb has many possibilities but most agree that the construction found in this text is making a positive affirmative statement of what has happened.

Fitzmyer and others point to the possibility that we might have in this pericope an early Christian confession of faith, one possibly related to baptism, or a possible baptismal chant or hymn.

---

[64] J. D. G. Dunn, J. D. G. *Romans 1–8*, Dallas: Word, Incorporated, 1998, p. 494 f.

[65] Robert H. Mounce, *Romans,* Nashville: Broadman and Holman Publishers, 1995, p. 189. Italics, IAF)

If this is true then Paul is simply affirming a confession that Christians have already made! *In Christ they have been predestined to be conformed to Christ!*

Paul makes reference the foreknowledge, predestination, calling, justification and glorification of the saints to assure them that at their baptism that God had done this. He had predestined them to justification and to be conformed to Christ. This was the confession they had made at their baptism. The purpose of this poetic confession would be to confirm the security of the saints and assure them that God has been working for them since before creation (the foreknowledge of God) and would not fail them in their difficult present. In God's eternal plan the saints were destined by God to be conformed to the image of his son, an eschatological concept, both a proleptic in the present and a final transformation at the end.

Rom 8:29 states clearly the purpose of God's predestination! "For those whom he foreknew he also predestined *to be conformed to the image of his Son ...*"

The point is that biblical predestination as referenced by Paul in this pericope was not to the personal salvation or damnation of a select few as is claimed by Calvinistic predestination, *but to a progressive eschatological transformation into the image of God's son, or into the image of their creator* (Eph 4:23; Col 3:10; 2 Cor 3:18).

Summary of Eph 1:3-12 and Rom 8:29, 30

These texts explain that God has an eternal plan, *determined before creation*, to *redeem those in Christ* who loved him and shared in his covenant relationship based on faith and to transform them into the image of his son.

This predetermined predestined plan was that *in Christ* the Christians, by faith in Christ, would be transformed into the likeness of Christ, God's son and bring glory to God in Christ and the church. God knew beforehand according to his foreknowledge that, certain things would occur and based on his foreknowledge he had decided to do something so Christians could be his children. He decided to send Jesus to die for the sins of all, and then called all to faith through the gospel message proclaiming the death, burial, and resurrection of Jesus who died for all. The heart of the gospel plan calls all people through faith to be transformed in Christ into the children of God.

This predestination is not simply a predestination to salvation but to being transformed daily and ultimately into the image of our creator; that image which we lost through sin and disobedience, not simply through Adam's sin, but through our own sin. We chose however to emulate the example of Adam to disobey God, and to be lost. In Christ God predestined us to be saved and transformed into the image of his son, Jesus, and not into the image of Adam, so that we could bring glory to God through Christ and the church.

Calvinistic Predestination holds that God arbitrarily decided beforehand that some persons (individuals) should be saved, and some persons (individuals) should be lost. Pauline and biblical predestination holds that based on his foreknowledge that man would sin God decided "beforehand" that Jesus would die for sin, and that through the faithfulness of Jesus and faith in Jesus believers in Christ would or could become His sons and be "conformed into his image".

Simply put Paul decrees that God predestined, decided beforehand, according to his foreknowledge that those in Christ would become his children and be transformed in to the image of Christ! This is a *corporate* predestination, not an *individual* predestination; it refers to those who love God and who are in Christ, *corporately*. We might claim that God knows before we would individually believe in Christ and that we would individually obey him and that we would individually become his children, and this is true, but the predestination, or predetermining Paul describes is a *corporate* one that proclaims that those in Christ would become transformed into Christ's image and become God's children.

Thus it is *corporately in Christ* that this takes place and this is what God had decided before creation!

Calvinistic Predestination[66]

Broadly speaking Calvinistic Predestination arose out of the Augustinian doctrine of Inherited Sin and Total Depravity.

According to these views man is born totally depraved since his image of God in which he was created was destroyed in the sin of Adam. Man at his birth inherits the sinful nature of Adam and is alienated from God by sin and has his being created in God's image either totally or seriously impaired.

This doctrine was early proclaimed by Augustine ca 400 A.D. and eventually adopted by John Calvin and the early Protestant Reformation.[67] It is defined variously by predestinarian groups.

Calvinistic (Reformed Theology) and Lutheran theology holds that in the fall of man (Adam's sin) man lost his image of God (*Imago Dei*) and has as a consequence lost the ability to reason and understand God fully. It is only through the direct action of the Holy Spirit that man can fully understand God and come to faith; faith thus is not man's working, but the work of the Holy Spirit. Luther held that unregenerate man can understand the outer clarity of Scripture, but without the Holy Spirit could not understand the inner meaning of the Scriptures. In the Calvinistic view God decided who of fallen men would be saved and who lost. All men in this view deserve to be lost and in God's sovereign freedom God can decide who to save and who not to save. We do not deny God's sovereign freedom to do as he wills but Calvinistic predestination is not what Paul explains God has decided to do!

---

[66] For studies in Calvinistic Predestination for the purposes of this study I recommend Alan Richardson, *A Dictionary of Christian Theology*. The topic is widely discussed in most major theological or biblical dictionaries. Cf. also Donald G. Bloesch, *Essentials of Evangelical Theology*, Vol. 2, and Donald Guthrie, *New Testament Theology*.

[67] Cf. Alan Richardson, *A Dictionary of Christian Theology*, "Doctrine of Man and Predestination".

Summary of Calvinistic Predestination under the Acronym TULIP

T represents total depravity and holds that every person is born inheriting Adam's sin and is therefore totally depraved and unable to understand God.

U represents unconditional election. God chose some to be saved and some to be lost as an arbitrary choice by his grace and we have no say in his choice since we all deserve condemnation for our sin.

L represents limited atonement. Jesus died only for the elect: those whom God has chosen. God limits his choice and calling.

I represents irresistible grace which means that when God chose and predestined a person to be saved he sends his Holy Spirit to bring about their faith and conversion. The elect cannot resist the working of the Holy Spirit.

P represents preservation of the saints. The Holy Spirit sees to it that the saved cannot fall away from grace. No matter what happens, the elect will get to heaven! It is this mindset that develops the doctrine held by some that once the saved are saved, they are always saved.

Classical Restoration Movement (Church of Christ and Christian Church) Thinking

Followers of the Restoration Movement, Church of Christ and Christian Church, obviously influenced by John Locke [ca. 1700] and Alexander Campbell [ca 1800], both classical rationalists, have traditionally and theologically held that the origin of faith in an individual is located in the belief that the Scriptures are rational and can be understood by rational man, even fallen man, and that through the study and conviction of the Scriptures, individuals can without the aid of the Holy Spirit come to know the Scriptures and come to faith and make the decision to repent and accept Christ.

Faith, then, according to this view results from an individual's *rational comprehension* of Scripture and a *decision* to accept that rational conclusion.

Although Campbell had an appreciation for the working of the Holy Spirit he would not accept the direct intervention and operation of the Holy Spirit on man in the initial development of faith in the individual. Faith had to be a rational conclusion to the evidence of Scripture.

Some of Campbell's followers took Campbell's views to the extreme and held that the only way the Holy Spirit ever works in one's life was exclusively through the Word. This may help us understand why some members of Churches of Christ have until recently had difficulty accepting the indwelling work of the Holy Spirit in that by doing so they may detract from a rational approach and comprehension of Scripture.

This is unfortunate and has led to a diminution of appreciation of the working of the Holy Spirit in the new birth and *maturation* of faith. It would have been better had members of the Church of Christ paid closer attention to Barton W. Stone, who although similar in approach to Campbell in a rational understanding of Scripture, also accepted the working of the Holy Spirit in the development of faith! Stone view was perhaps a more balanced approach than that adopted by Campbell's extreme rationalist followers!

Several Scriptures however Support the Conclusion that Faith Results from the Hearing, Learning, and Comprehension of Scripture

In 2 Tim 3:14-16 Paul wrote to Timothy his young disciple encouraging him to remain firm in his faith.

> " *But as for you, continue in what you have learned and have firmly believed, knowing from whom you learned it* [15] *and how from childhood you have been acquainted with the sacred writings which are able to instruct you for salvation through faith in Christ Jesus.*
> "[16] *All scripture is inspired by God and profitable for teaching, for reproof, for correction, and for training in righteousness,* [17] *that the man of God may be complete, equipped for every good work."*

Likewise at 2 Tim 2:15 Paul wrote, "Do your best to present yourself to God as one approved, a workman who has no need to be ashamed, *rightly handling the word of truth ...*"

On the same topic Paul wrote concerning a disobedient Israel at Rom 10:16, "Lord, who has believed what he has heard from us?" [17] So *faith comes from what is heard, and what is heard comes by the preaching of Christ.*"

Note particularly John 5: 39: "You search the scriptures, because you think that in them you have eternal life; and *it is they that bear witness to me ...*"

Also John 20:30, 31,

> *"Now Jesus did many other signs in the presence of the disciples, which are not written in this book;* [31] *but these are written that you may believe that Jesus is the Christ, the Son of God, and that believing you may have life in his name."*

It seems obvious that Scripture, and an appropriate understanding of Scripture, has a large part to play in the development and maturation of faith, but this does not exclude prayer and the working of God, the Holy Spirit, and biblical teaching in the development and maturation of faith.

The issue or difference between a Restoration Movement (Church of Christ) view of faith and that of Luther/Calvinism relates to their divergent views regarding the relationship between man's unregenerate mind (Luther and Calvin) and faith and man's rational ability to understand Scripture and the Gospel of Christ. Lutheranism/Calvinism holds that unregenerate man cannot understand the Scriptures so as to bring them to saving faith. Those in the Restoration Movement (Churches of Christ, Christian Church) do not accept the negative anti-rational Luther/Calvinistic views[68] of man's total depravity and loss of the *Imago Dei*. Restorationists adhere to man's rational capability (as in Paul), and man's ability to understand Scripture

---

[68] One should recognize that Lutheran and Calvinistic views are not monolithic and that what is being described as Lutheran/Calvinistic is a broad definition of these views.

and the saving message of Jesus Christ. Restoration thinkers do not reject the work of the Holy Spirit in the maturing of faith but hold that man's rational capacity is adequate for understand the rational nature of Scripture in bringing man to understand God's saving grace and faith in the death, burial, and resurrection of Jesus.

Radical Calvinism holds that without the *initial direct operation* of the Holy Spirit man cannot reason adequately and consequently cannot unaided by the Holy Spirit believe, for man is primarily totally depraved and has lost the Image of God which Calvinism relates to rationality!

Moderate Lutheranism holds that *without the assistance of the Holy Spirit one is not able to understand the inner meaning of Scripture*. One can read and understand the outer nature of Scripture but not receive the inner regenerating power of Scripture without the assistance of the Holy Spirit. Both Luther and Calvin held that man's *imago dei*, the *image of God*, which is his rational reasoning nature, was destroyed or seriously impaired by Adam's fall. Man inherits this impaired or lost *imago dei* "gene" either in birth, through parents who have lost their *imago dei*, or through man's corrupt and impaired mind.

Both Calvin and Luther held to the importance of Scripture but in addition held that without *the direct intervention of the Holy Spirit* one would not be able to understand the inner regenerative nature of Scripture which brings one to a redeeming faith in Jesus. In the Reformed Calvinistic and Lutheran theology of Scripture, and *sola scriptura*[69], it is held that without

---

[69] *Sola Scriptura* can be variously defined but primarily stand in opposition to human interpretation and the church's right to define faith ... the key implication of the principle is that interpretations and applications of the Scriptures do not have the same authority as the Scriptures themselves; hence, ecclesiastical authority is viewed as subject to correction by the Scriptures, even by an individual member of the Church. Luther said, "A simple layman armed with Scripture is greater than the mightiest pope without it". The intention of the Reformation was to correct the perceived errors of the Catholic Church by appeal to the uniqueness of the Bible's authority and to reject what Catholics considered to be Apostolic Tradition as a source of

the direct involvement of the Holy Spirit Scripture cannot either be properly understood or that it lies beyond unregenerate man's irrational comprehension.

In my PhD dissertation on *Wolfhart Pannenberg's theology as a Reaction to Dialectical Theology: Carl Barth and Rudolf Bultmann* (University of KwaZulu-Natal, South Africa) I trace the thought of Barth in which he stresses the direct operation of the Holy Spirit in the creation of faith, and Bultmann who stressed an exegetical experience in the creation of faith. Barth's and Bultmann's primary objection was of history being an adequate source of faith. Pannenberg rejected both approaches and stressed a rational approach to Scripture in the creation of faith, which conclusion I supported.

I am referring the reader also to an Abilene Christian University College of Biblical Studies faculty discussion of three positions adopted by different approaches to Biblical theology and faith regarding man and the role of reason and the Holy Spirit.

One view is that there are those who have a *low* estimate of man's potential and a high estimate of Holy Spirit intervention (Calvin and Luther).

Then there is the view that holds to a *high* estimate of man's potential and a low estimate of Scripture and the working of the Holy Spirit (classical liberalism and some post- modern views).

Finally, there is the median view of Restoration Movement estimates regarding the relationship between man's *high rational ability* and a *high estimate of Scripture* and the *operation of the Holy Spirit*. This view holds that man through his high rational ability has a high view of Scripture which he can understand and

---

original authority alongside the Bible ... *Sola Scriptura* ... sees the Bible as the only final authority in matters of faith and practice. As Luther once said, "The true rule is this: God's Word shall establish articles of faith, and no one else, not even an angel can do so ..." This summary is drawn from comments from Wikipedia, *Sola Scriptura*, and is intended only to be a guide to understanding the general doctrine of Sola Scriptura.

believe. One may then call on the Holy Spirit to help one understand how to apply Scripture to religious faith, life, and maturity.

(See diagram on following page)

Low – Median – High Views of Man and the Holy Spirit
in the Development of Faith

Low estimate of man.
High estimate of Holy
Spirit intervention.
Calvin and Luther.

Reasonable estimate of
man.
High estimate of
Scripture and the
operation of the Holy
Spirit.
Restoration Theology.

High estimate of man.
Low estimate of
Scripture and Holy
Spirit intervention.
*Classical Liberalism
and some Post-modern
views.*

Lesson 5b
The Origin and Cycle of Faith/Trust
Introduction

In the origin and development of faith as *saving faith* or *trust* there are four elements, *one*, information (*notitia*, to take notice), *two*, knowledge (*assensus* the acceptance of that information), *three*, trust (*fiducia*, the decision to act on that information or knowledge), and *four*, the cycle of returning to reexamine the information and build on it from a deeper understanding of the information, *notitia*, of Scripture.[70]

Notitia. *Notitia* refers to the *content* of faith, or *information* that we believe. We place our faith in something, for example, Scripture. We examine Scripture to determine whether it is sound or reliable.

Assensus. *Assensus* is our *decision to accept* the *information* provided by Scripture which becomes *knowledge* or *Assensus*. We give our *assent to*, or *accept* the information. But one can know about the Christian faith from Scripture and yet decide to do nothing about that knowledge. You might believe it to be true, but not act on it. Many people believe in Jesus, they accept the information regarding Jesus, but ignore him as the Lord that Scripture teaches. Jesus is just part of the knowledge (*Assensus*) one gains from the information one accepts, (the *Notitia* or information gained from Scripture). We might even believe that knowledge to be true, but not be willing to act on it. That is not saving faith or trust (*Fiducia*). Saving faith or *Fiducia* derives from a wilful decision to accept and act on the knowledge we have. The knowledge may not be perfect or completely

---

[70] This cycle is adapted from information from Wolfhart Pannenberg, *Basic Questions and Answers*, Vol. 2, Philadelphia; Fortress Press, 1971, pp. 30 ff; Ian A. Fair, *Wolfhart Pannenberg's Reaction to Dialectical Theology*, PhD dissertation, University of KwaZulu-Natal, 1975; E. Frank Tupper, *The Theology of Wolfhart Pannenberg*, Philadelphia; The Westminster Press, 1972, pp. 122 ff.

understood, but that is what faith is, it is a decision to accept the knowledge we gain from evidence such as Scripture.

Fiducia. *Fiducia* or *trust* results from the decision to accept and act upon the evidence of Scripture. This leads to *personal trust* and reliance. Knowing and believing the content of the Christian faith is not enough, for even demons can do that (James 2:19). Faith is only effectual if, knowing about and assenting to the claims of Jesus, one personally trusts (*Fiducia*) in Him for salvation.

The Cycle of Faith. Faith often begins slowly and may begin as an immature faith and trust, but one returns to the source of the faith, the *Notitia* which is Scripture and continues to examine Scripture and its teachings and implications, learning more and growing in one's knowledge of the faith.

Lesson 5c
Diagram of the Origin and Maturing of Saving Faith/Trust

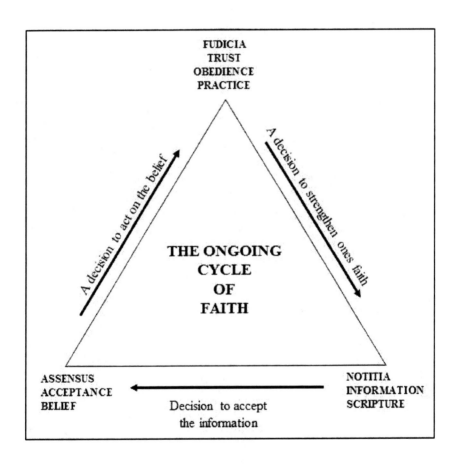

FUDICIA
TRUST
OBEDIENCE
PRACTICE

A decision to act on the belief

A decision to strengthen ones faith

THE ONGOING
CYCLE
OF
FAITH

ASSENSUS
ACCEPTANCE
BELIEF

NOTITIA
INFORMATION
SCRIPTURE

Decision to accept
the information

HCU MEDIA LLC
Publishing in support of
Heritage Christian University – Ghana (HCU Ghana)
www.hcuc.edu.gh

HCU media has been established to support the publication of materials, both paper and electronic, created by faculty and friends of HCU Ghana. These materials are available globally.

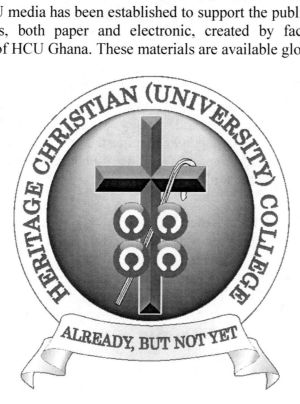

HCU Ghana (www.hcuc.edu.gh) is a Christian Liberal Arts University begun by the leadership of the Nsawam Rd. Church of Christ in Accra, Ghana with the assistance of many people, most notably the George Chisholm family and the faculty of Abilene Christian University. (www.acu.edu).

Commencing September 2014, HCU Ghana will offer degrees accredited by the Ghanaian national Accreditation Board (NAB) and consequently, internationally accredited bachelor degrees; in Theology, Business (Accounting, Finance, Human Resource Management, Marketing) and Information Science & Technology. HCU Ghana is affiliated with Kwame Nkrumah University of Science & Technology (www.knust.edu.gh).

Heritage Christian College Foundation USA (HCCF USA www.hccf-usa.org**)** was established in 2008 as a 501(c) 3 non-profit foundation with the purpose of providing donors the ability to provide needed seed capital and scholarship funding to the university. HCU Ghana intends to

be a self-funding university however in order to provide educations to needy students, scholarship funds are needed; most scholarship candidates will be orphans and ministry majors. Additionally, funding facilities requires the help of donors so that the costs of facilities do not become a burden to the tuition cost.

HCU Media LLC (www.HCUMedia.com) is the first of many entrepreneurial efforts sponsored by HCU Ghana. HCU Media is the "university press" for HCU Ghana. It will initially have offices in

Plano, TX., USA and in Accra, Ghana. It will publish materials both paper and electronic which are intended to be an outlet for faculty and friends and to provide funding to the university when possible.

Coming soon from
HCU Media in early 2014!

Kingdom Theology

This will be available in Paperback and Kindle eBook forms.

To receive notification of availability, please send an email to sales@HCUMedia.com with your request.

About our Author

Ian A. Fair (PhD)
Professor Emeritus of New Testament
and New Testament Theology
Graduate School of Theology
College of Biblical Studies
Abilene Christian University

TEACHING & SPECIALIZATION	SEMINARS AND WORKSHOPS
Revelation	Revelation
Romans	Romans
Prison Epistles	Matthew
Synoptic Gospels:	Strategic Planning
Matthew	Leadership
1 & 2 Thessalonians	Unity in Diversity
Leadership	

Education
Ph.D. in Systematic Theology, University of Natal, South Africa
Dissertation: *The Theology of Wolfhart Pannenberg as a Reaction to Dialectical Theology*
MA in New Testament Theology, University of Natal, South Africa
Thesis: *The Resurrection of Jesus in Three Contemporary Theologians*
BA Honors in Bible and Theology, University of Natal, South Africa
BA in Bible, Abilene Christian University, Abilene, Texas, USA
Diploma in Civil Engineering, Witswatersrand Technical College, South Africa

Dr. Fair is serving as Interim Dean for the School of Theology at HCU Ghana pending the transfer of this role to a Ghanaian Scholar.

CPSIA information can be obtained at www.ICGtesting.com
Printed in the USA
LVOW13s1226260114

370852LV00003BB/6/P